"Don't even think about hiring a ghostwriter until you read this book. Mahesh Grossman's easy to follow, smart advice will save you time and help you avoid costly mistakes. The only good reason to skip this book is if you hire Mahesh."

Dan Poynter
Author of *The Self-Publishing Manual*

"This book is so good, you should buy 10 and give it to all your friends who want to be published."

Dottie Walters
Author of *Speak and Grow Rich*

"Mahesh Grossman takes all the mystery out of hiring a ghostwriter and getting your book into print! This guide is thorough, well-organized, enjoyably written, and packed with genuinely useful information!"

Susan Page
Author of *The Shortest Distance Between You and a Published Book*

"Mahesh Grossman offers solid information about how authoring a book can enhance your professional reputation, and how hiring a ghostwriter can help speed up and smooth out the process."

Jennifer Basye Sander
Author of *The Complete Idiot's Guide to Getting Published*
Former Senior Editor, Random House

"Immensely valuable . . .Whether you're a pauper or a king, Mahesh Grossman shows you how to hire a ghostwriter who fits your budget. With your own ghostwriter, you'll feel just like a celebrity. Follow the instructions in Grossman's insightful book, and pretty soon you might be one!"

Rick Frishman
President of Planned Television Arts
And author of *Guerrilla Publicity* and
Guerrilla Marketing for Writers

"You really can write a book without lifting a finger. Feel queasy about having someone else do the hard work? Grossman will talk you out of your qualms. Not sure how to find a ghostwriter or how much to pay him or her? He covers all the ins and outs of this, and much, much more. Highly recommended."

Marcia Yudkin
Author of *Six Steps to Free Publicity* and 10 other books

"The second part of this book shows you the same formula I used to sell my book for a six-figure advance. If you want to be taken seriously by agents and publishers, you need to get your hands on this book."

Rich Fettke
Author of *Extreme Success*

"In his masterful 'Write a Book Without Lifting a Finger,' Mahesh Grossman tells truths that many authors never want you to know. But everything he says is right on the button. His book is very easy to read and extremely valuable for anyone who has ever fantasized about seeing their name on a real published book. It's obvious to me that Mr. Grossman lifted all ten fingers to write such an enlightening book."

Jay Conrad Levinson
Author, *Guerrilla Marketing* series of books
Over 14 million copies sold; now in 39 languages

"Drop everything and read this book. I'm serious. I've never seen this much good information presented so concisely, cogently and usefully. Oh, and by the way, if you intend to sell your services as a business owner, consultant or speaker, there is no better advertisement you can get for yourself than a published book!"

David Garfinkel
Author, *Advertising Headlines That Make You Rich*

Write a Book
Without
Lifting a Finger

By Mahesh Grossman

10 Finger Press   -   Santa Cruz, CA

Printed in the United States of America

ISBN: 0-9728131-0-1

**Publisher's Cataloging-in-Publication
(Provided by Quality Books, Inc.)**

Grossman, Mahesh.
    Write a book without lifting a finger / by Mahesh Grossman.
    p.cm.
    Includes bibliographical references.
    LCCN 2003093812
    ISBN 0-9728131-0-1

    1. Ghostwriting.   I. Title.

PN171.G47G76 2003   808'.02
                          QBI03-200459

We possess the wealth of words,
With weapons of words we will fight;
Words are the breath of our life,
We will distribute the wealth of words among the people;
Tuka says, Look! The meaning of the Word is God,
With the Word we will extol and worship.

Tukaram

ACKNOWLEDGEMENTS

To the One who created thoughts, words, and writing.

I humbly offer my thanks to His Holiness Sri Sri Ganapathi Sachchidananda, my beloved spiritual teacher and so much more.

My wife Uma and my daughter Manasa put up with both a missing dad and husband and a temperamental deadline-frenzied fiend during the writing of this book. I thank them for all their love and forgiveness through the process of writing this book.

Chris Psaros has assisted me in every way possible on this book (including pulling an all-nighter so my e-book would be available on the morning of my radio tour). He laid out its interior, too. Chris has also designed my web pages and brochures, helped me with my business and entertained my daughter when she was bored. There is no thank you equal to all you have done for me, Chris, but thank you nonetheless.

Jay Conrad Levinson gave me my first blurb for this book when I was only a quarter of the way done. Nothing helps you feel like a soon-to-be-published author like a testimonial from a guy who has sold over 14 million books. Thanks for helping this project feel real at a time when it seemed more like a pipe dream.

Marcia Yudkin gave me some good advice along the way.

Special thanks to the ghostwriters, authors, agents, editors and publicists who let me interview them, including Rick Wolff, Ed Tivnan, Mark Steissel, Robert Shepard, Rob Wise, Susan Campbell, Rob Woodcox, and Mark Chimsky.

Profound gratitude to the authors who lent me their book proposals as well as contributing other vital information to this book; Rich Fettke, Cindy Ventrice, Peggy Vincent, Allen Klein, Barbara Bartlein, and Diane Dreher.

Thanks to David Garfinkel and Matthew Samp for their suggestions in writing the back cover.

To my Borders buddies who helped me edit early drafts: Rob Ellis, Jay Olsen and John. Thanks, guys.

Vincent and Fred Nardi gave me my first ghostwriting job. Adrienne Ingrum was my first editor. Sherri Robb and Bart Andrews were my first agents. Thanks to all of them for teaching me about the publishing business.

A special thanks to my parents and my sister for a lifetime of love and support.

CONTENTS

SECTION III
SAMPLE BOOK PROPOSALS

We should be taught not to wait for inspiration to start a thing.

Action always generates inspiration.

Inspiration seldom generates action.

- Frank Tibolt

THREE TRUE STORIES

The streets of New York City were gray and covered with slush, around Christmas in 1985, when I got to know a young man from South Africa. His name was Martin. We were both a little past college age. We met while we were moonlighting for the Metropolitan Opera. Despite the venue, the work wasn't glamorous. We spent our evenings on the phone, asking members of the Metropolitan Opera Guild to renew their annual donations.

By 1985, apartheid had become big news. This despicable brand of segregation had only recently entered the American public's awareness, so any story about the sad plight of blacks in South Africa was worthy of media attention. I was fascinated whenever Martin was willing to talk with me about life in his homeland.

Like many people in his native country, Martin had attended a segregated school, one that was more crowded, had poorer facilities and fewer books than the schools attended by the white minority. That's what all the schools for blacks were like.

One night we had dinner with a friend of mine who was the editor-in-chief for a publishing house. Martin mentioned that he was beginning a treatise on his experience in South Africa. My publisher friend was very encouraging. He thought Martin had a story to tell that was relevant and unique. Many people would be responsive to an inside look at a South African school for blacks during apartheid. What made Martin's experience even more inspiring was that he wasn't forced to attend this school. He *volunteered* to go there. How did he happen to have a choice in this matter? Martin was <u>white</u>!

You don't need to be the head of a publishing house to know that Martin's memoirs, even if they turned out terribly, would be a publicist's dream. When your life story intersects with an ongoing news story, every TV and radio show in America wants you.

It's amazing to me that almost twenty years later, though our friendship was brief, I still recall Martin's story. You would remember it too, if you had seen him on television or read his book.

But you didn't. *Martin*, in spite of a compelling tale and a supportive acquaintance in the publishing industry, *never actually wrote it.*

In 1986, at Sandy Levy's seminar, *The Art of Personal Marketing*, I met a man who had worked for three different car dealerships. He planned to work for one more dealer, and then write about what he learned. Armed with the sales policies of all the major auto brands, he would be able to tell consumers everything they would need to know to get a great price on a car.

What a great approach for a book! Whenever I buy a car, I wonder how much money I would have saved if he had actually written it.

This last story has a happier ending. It's about a doctor who worked with his city's Police Benevolent Society. Dr. Lager (not his real name) became as much of a psychologist as a physician to local cops who suffered from the vast pressures of police life. He started working with them on issues like diet, mindset, and coping skills as a way of keeping from getting sick. Eventually, he realized that he had developed a system that could help people stay well by teaching them to deal with their emotions.

For many years Dr. Lager thought about writing a book. When the Internet came along, he searched for a ghostwriter. After calling a few, he chose Robert Woodcox. Dr. Lager and Robert spent a year 'writing' over the phone, sometimes having conversations that lasted five hours.

When they finished, Robert called a small firm that had published one of his previous efforts and asked them to read it. Less than a year later, Dr. Lager's book was in bookstores.

THE PURPOSE OF THIS BOOK

Dr. Lager's story is extremely unusual in one respect. Ordinarily, it's not that easy to get published.

Then again, he had the right qualifications. He was an expert writing about his life's work.

It also helped that he had a manuscript.

How many great ideas go unpublished because they were never written at all?

How many people can fill a book, but lack the time, the skill, or the persistence to write one?

How many potential authors could eventually see their work in print with the help of a ghostwriter?

I'm guessing thousands.

The trouble is, it doesn't even occur to most regular people to hire one.

And folks who consider working with a ghostwriter often have concerns that keep them from following through on the idea. Maybe you're one of those people.

You may think that, even with a ghostwriter, it takes too much time to write a book. But the truth is most ghostwriters only need **five to ten hours per month** of your time in order to create your opus—in four to six months.

You may assume you have to be rich to afford a ghostwriter.

Interviews with writers, statistics spread throughout this book, and my own memory of charging far less than I was worth after I had been published, show that you can hire an experienced writer for as little as $500 to write enough of your book so that you'll land a publishing contract.

And there are talented up and coming writers who will charge you less than that.

You may be puzzled about how to find ghostwriters, judge their work and evaluate their costs.

You've come to the right place. This volume will end your bewilderment.

At least I hope so.

In order to write this book, I've drawn from a unique combination of experiences. My thirteen years as a Silicon Valley headhunter taught me the ins and outs of looking for people who are hard to find—just like ghostwriters. My ghostwriting experience on a number of books issued by major New York publishing houses give me inside knowledge of the publishing industry and an understanding of the mindset of ghostwriters. Of course, my experience on a couple of ghostwriting fiascos lends me first-hand knowledge of what to avoid when collaborating on a book.

WRITE A BOOK WITHOUT LIFTING A FINGER tells you why even a gifted scribe should hire a ghostwriter. It will give you permission - and the means - to recruit someone to help you with your book, no matter what your budget. It shows you what to put on paper in order to approach literary agents and publishers. And it points out pitfalls that can occur along the way as well as details your contract must include so that you and your unique information are protected.

If you need some help starting (or finishing) that book you want to publish, PAY ATTENTION. You may be just a helping hand away from a bestseller!

SECTION I
HOW TO HIRE A GHOSTWRITER EVEN IF YOU'RE ON A SHOESTRING BUDGET

WHAT IS A GHOSTWRITER?

The publishing industry has a very specific meaning for the word 'ghostwriter'. A ghostwriter is someone who gets paid to write a book that is published under another person's name. The "author" is usually a celebrity whose name will sell books. Depending on the circumstances, the author contributes anything from all the information, as in an autobiography, to practically none of it, as sometimes occurs with diet and exercise books.

You may be writing a book where you don't need to appear to be the sole author. Perhaps you just want someone to write with. If you give your co-writer credit on the cover or title page of the book, publishers will refer to her as a co-author or a second author.

How to determine what credit, if any, you offer to your collaborator is discussed extensively in Chapter 10.

For the rest of this book, though, the term "ghostwriter" is used as a generic term for your co-writer. Negotiate whether her name goes on the cover after you decide you want to hire her.

(One quick note: For the rest of this book, when indefinite pronouns are required, I will do my best to balance the "hes and hims" with the "shes and hers".)

WHAT DOES A GHOSTWRITER DO?

A ghostwriter works differently with every client. Depending on
a) the type of working relationship you want b) how much you've written when you hire him, and c) how much experience he has, a ghostwriter can help you do some, or all, of the following:

1) Brainstorm the title of your book.
2) Define the audience you are writing for. The readers of *The National Enquirer* and *The New Yorker* expect very different writing styles. So do the folks who imbibe *Ms.* and the *Ladies Home Journal.*
3) Create an angle to make your book different from the other books on the subject.
4) Find out what subset of your encyclopedia-like knowledge would make the best book. (Instead of *Everything You Need to Know about Selling Cars*, you might be guided to: *Taking the High Road: Earn More Money as a High Integrity, Win-Win Car Salesman.*)
5) Determine the size of your market.
6) Create an outline.

7) Provide research and interviews to support your suppositions.
8) Write your whole manuscript from scratch. Talk into a tape recorder and let her take notes, then she takes your information and adds introductions, transitions and summaries. You literally won't lift a finger.
9) Share the writing with you.
10) Rewrite your material to increase its clarity and improve its style.
11) Coax you to provide anecdotes to illustrate your concepts.
12) Tell you to keep half of what you've written, throw out the rest and add significant new material.
13) Create a sample of your book, your biography, and the marketing materials a publisher wants to see so that you can sell a book before you write it.
14) Write query letters to publishers and agents, and then submit book samples to those who were interested in your idea.

But If I Use a Ghost, What's My Job?

Maybe you're wondering, 'how can I feel like it's my book if a ghostwriter is doing all the work?'

Relax. It's still your book. You can share any of the tasks listed above if you want. Or you can sit back and let your writer handle them. Even if you choose not to lift a finger, you are still the author. Why?

Because it's *your* knowledge that at the center of this book. *Your* experience creates the material. *You* are the reason this book exists.

If you hire an accountant to do your taxes, should he get all the credit for the success of your business?

Besides, when the book is published, you will have plenty to do. You are the face behind the book. You will have to promote it, give interviews, go on book tours, give speeches, etc. While you're waiting for the bellhop at yet another Holiday Inn, your ghostwriter will be typing away on someone else's project.

You, not your writer, are the one who knows your subject well enough to answer questions on it. Can your writer share many appropriate anecdotes that aren't in the book? Not really.

It's not his life experience that provides the material. It's yours.

How many years has it taken for you to acquire this information?
That's your contribution. And it's GIGANTIC!

What If a Ghostwriter Steals My Idea?

Here's a little secret from inside the publishing industry. An idea that isn't already successful won't get stolen.

An idea that is making money, however, will be pilfered over and over again.

Write a how-to book about building bird feeders that starts a bird feeder craze and sells 100,000 books, and soon you'll see *Bird Feeders for Dummies, The Idiot's Guide To Building Bird Feeders*, and *the Everything Bird Feeder Book*, to name just a few. In addition to these branded how-to books, there will be others that are blatant copies of yours, but with better covers, sexier titles, and color illustrations.

Even if your idea were to be stolen by a ghostwriter, what good would it do her? To sell a non-fiction book, the author must be a credible expert on its subject matter. A ghostwriter doesn't have experience in your field. She doesn't have your anecdotes and she hasn't spent the hours you've spent thinking about this subject. If she did, she'd be working on a similar book without you!

Don't let your worry that someone is going to come along and steal your idea keep you from hiring a ghostwriter. *Instead, be afraid of anything that is going to stop you from completing your book.*

CHAPTER 2

A GHOSTWRITING EPIDEMIC

This is how prevalent ghostwriters are:

I recently attended a wonderful workshop with Nina Wise, a performance artist who uses movement as a point of departure for improvising stories on stage. Her work is full of texture as she instantaneously describes small moments like flipping through silk cloths at a mercantile center. The painstaking details she improvises would take mere mortals hours of rewrites to achieve. Her writing is absolutely poetic when she has the time to polish it. Here's an example:

> "In the same way that birds sing, and lions roar, and prairie dogs dance, and cicadas chant, and water sculpts rock, and sunsets paint the sky, we, too, are of the nature to sing, and roar, and dance, and chant, and sculpt, and paint."

Nina came down to Santa Cruz to promote her newly minted book, *A Big New Free Happy Unusual Life.* Nina told us that four publishers bid on her book, which she wrote with her own two hands. Even though she is a noted storyteller, all four wanted to know who her ghostwriter was. 'Whoever it was,' they said, 'did a fabulous job of capturing your voice.'

Maybe they should have read her bio one more time.

CONJUNCTIONS 101

Before we discuss ghostwriters, though, let's talk about collaborators. A collaborator is a writer who gets credit on the front of the book.

Take a minute to walk through your bookstore.

Pick up a book with two authors on the cover. If both writers are listed in the same size type with the word "and" between their names, they are usually collaborators with the same stature. They are both equally responsible for the book and both are referred to as its authors. The authors of *The Nanny Diaries*, Emma McLaughlin and Nicola Kraus, fall into this category.

However, if one author listed is in bigger type than the other, separated by the word "and", the one in bigger type is the author, the name in smaller print is that of the co-author or second author. The second author could have contributed ideas to the book or she may be just a writer. You have to look at the authors biographies on the back inside flap to tell, but usually, the bigger the second author's name appears on the cover of a book, the more likely she is to have contributed ideas, and not just writing skill, to a book.

It's easier to tell who did what if writers use a different approach.

When two authors are separated by the word "with", the ideas or the story in the book are normally those of the one listed first. The second writer has usually just taken the author's story or ideas and made them publishable. This format is used when the author is a celebrity. *It's Not About the Bike* is by Tour de France winner Lance Armstrong *with* Sally Jenkins. *Let's Roll* is by Lisa Beamer, wife of September 11th Hero Todd Beamer, *with* Ken Abraham.

Occasionally, writers manipulate the credits for their own reasons. Hal Zina Bennett and Michael Larsen, authors of *How to Write with a Collaborator*, contributed equally to the book but Hal's name is in bigger print and their names are separated by the word "with".

Here's why: They wanted Bennett to promote the book, while Larsen, a literary agent, stayed home. With equal billing, if Bennett appeared on television without Larsen, the host and the audience might feel slighted. With this arrangement, no one was the wiser.

Do these distinctions really matter? To many editors, writers and agents within the publishing industry, the answer is yes. However, the general public doesn't give a flying Flahooly.

Neither does *The New York Times*.

The late reporter Dick Schaap wrote at least a dozen books "with" sports celebrities like Joe Namath, Joe Montana and Bo Jackson. His name appeared on the cover of every book he collaborated on. But when the Times reviewed Schaap's autobiography, *Flashing Before My Eyes,* guess what they used as the headline? "King of the Ghostwriters".

Soon it may be your turn to decide how to credit your collaborator. Remember, in most cases, being generous won't hurt you. It may actually be good for your image! And it will definitely be good for his career.

GHOST TEST YOUR BOOKSTORE

Many people, however, cling to the more traditional belief that the whole point of using a ghost is so that a book looks like only one person wrote it.

Out of gratitude, though, or perhaps contractual arrangement, many authors use the acknowledgements section to thank their unseen collaborators.

The way to "ghost test" a book is to read the author's acknowledgements carefully. This section used to always be in the front of a book, but these days, it is sometimes hidden in the back. Some authors explicitly mention a ghostwriter's contributions. Others are more secretive and may even use logic-defying euphemisms.

Here are samples from a variety of authors:

Almost everyone knows Dr. Phil (MacGraw), a psychologist who became famous when Oprah gave him a weekly slot to "tell it like it is" to members of her audience. She now produces his daily television show. Dr. Phil works with ghostwriter Jonathan Leach on most of his books. In *Self Matters*, Dr. Phil was wonderfully generous in his description of Leach's contribution to his works:

> "Thanks to Jonathan Leach for the writing and organizational skills
> brought to bear on this book. I have yet to write a single page in this or

my other books that Jonathan has not rubbed, scrubbed, massaged, and made exponentially better."

Dr. Phil was even more direct about his working relationship with Leach in the acknowledgements to his first treatise, *Life Strategies*: "Beyond undangling my participles and organizing my stream of consciousness, Jon contributed to the content of this book from his heart and mind."

Content implies at least some ghostwriting was involved.

But there's a reason that Dr. Phil doesn't take the leap and put Jonathan Leach's name on the cover, after three books together.

He doesn't want to disappoint his fans.

A Dr. Phil fan wouldn't want to think that some of the advice she is following was written, not by her favorite talk show psychologist, but by his ghostwriter.

Here's another case:

When a book bears the name of a trusted anchorman, you want to believe that he wrote every last word. But did he really?

The cover of *The American Dream* conveys the idea NBC's Dan Rather wrote it on his own. But look at how he acknowledges his agent, Bill Adler:

"He was a key part of the book's creation, and he guided, directed, and nurtured the germ of an idea all the way through to publication."

Sounds suspiciously like writing. But we need a little more evidence.

Let's hit the web for a little "power ghost testing".

How? A simple search on Google using an author's name and the word "ghostwriter" will reveal any public knowledge as to whether or not a book was ghostwritten.

If you search using "Dan Rather" AND "ghostwriter", you reach a link to http://www.ratherbiased.com. As you might guess, it's a site devoted to criticizing Dan Rather. Here's what it says:

"The fallout from Dan Rather's headlining of a Democratic fund-raiser in Texas continued this week. *Wall Street Journal* Opinion columnist, Peggy Noonan, cheekily says Rather should be commended for no longer pretending he has no opinions. She also tells how as the ghostwriter for his 'Dan Rather Reporting' column, 'it was starting to be a problem for me to write his point of view well' as she became more conservative."

If you used a ghostwriter for your 800 word column, it's very likely you used one for your 75,000 word book.

Rather is not the only TV newsman to obscure his use of a ghostwriter. In *Now Let Me Tell You What I Really Think*, MSNBC's Chris Matthews thanks Meaghan Nolan "for her diligence in organizing this book". Then he thanks Michele Slung "for the force and clarity of her editing."

If Meaghan Nolan only organized Matthews' book, what would he need editor Michele Slung for? "Organizing" is usually a code word authors use to acknowledge their ghostwriters.

Switching the television dial to the Sci-Fi channel, psychic John Edward is extremely generous in his acknowledgements for his book *Crossing Over.*

> "I want to express my thanks to Rick Firstman, not only for his collaboration on this book, but also for the energy and skill he poured into *One Last Time* [Edward's previous book] . . . Rick's ability to fashion my thoughts and experiences into an absorbing narrative have made it possible for me to share my story."

You may find it strange that Edward thanks Firstman for work on a previous book in *Crossing Over.* But look at the acknowledgements to One *Last Time*; Firstman isn't ever mentioned. So even to a somewhat educated observer, it looks like *Crossing Over* was written solely by John Edward.

There are many cases where you can't tell a book was ghostwritten. John F. Kennedy's *Profiles in Courage* won the Pulitzer Prize and had some effect in propelling him toward the presidency. It bears only his name on the cover and has no acknowledgements section.

Even when reporters asked Kennedy point blank whether he had any help with the book, he said no.

However, Herbert Parmet's biography of the president and other sources state that it was primarily written by future Kennedy speechwriter Theodore Sorenson and *New York Times* journalist Arthur Krock, Jr. To this day they receive 50% of the book's royalties.

ACTUAL STATISTICS

If you still feel uncomfortable about the idea of partnering with a ghostwriter, look at these statistics:

According to estimates by the *Times of London*, there are 120,000 new books published annually in the United States. That number is growing every year.

Of these, roughly 102,000, or 85%, are non-fiction.

Ghostwriting statistics are typically hard to pin down. Claudia Suzanne said this in WritersWeekly.com:

> "Book industry insiders estimate that 50% or more of all traditionally published books in today's market are worked on by one or more ghost . . . In the self-publishing world, the percentage is probably even higher."

Let's assume just half of the non-fiction published each year is written using additional writers. If you do the math, that's 51,000 books!

That number may be larger, if you believe Jack Hitt's comments in the *New York Times Magazine*:

"On any given week, up to half of any nonfiction best-seller list is written by someone other than the name on the book. Add those authors who . . . bury the writer's name in the acknowledgments, and the percentage, according to one agent, reaches as high as eighty."

What does this tell you?

If you use a ghostwriter, you are not alone. You may actually be in the majority.

And whether you are a housewife, a doctor, or a celebrity, your chance of getting published, or even better, of having a bestseller, actually increases when you use a collaborator.

CHAPTER 3

DO YOU NEED A GHOST?

Everybody needs a ghostwriter. Well, almost everybody.

And if you are writing because you want to land more clients at higher prices, or you want to change something about the world, or to get speaking engagements and media appearances and the revered status and lovely perks that many authors receive, you should be first in line to hire a ghostwriter.7

Why? I'll explain in a little bit.

First, I want you to fully comprehend the **CLOUT** a published book offers when you market your products, your services, or yourself.

AUTHOR POWER

Jay Conrad Levinson is famous as the author of the *Guerilla Marketing* series of books, which have sold over fourteen million copies and have been translated into thirty-nine languages. His pay for his first book (written years before he created *Guerilla Marketing*) wasn't close to that of his future successes. Jay says it offered other rewards:

> "I got a $15,000 advance, but it opened so many doors, to so many places I never even thought of going before. I'd say that in ten years, it earned a million dollars for me."

I asked Jay how a book opens doors. His answer was quite poetic:

> "For some strange reason people equate expertise with the written word. And, they think if you had it published, it's going to be right . . .
>
> If you wanted to work with a client and said that you're an expert in so and so, they'll either say yes or say no, but if you say 'and I've published a book on the topic,' they'll probably say yes.
>
> If you want to get to see somebody and make an appointment, you can write them a letter, maybe they'll say yes, maybe they'll say no. But if you write them a letter offering them a copy of the book you've written and you hand them a signed copy when you meet with them, chances are they'll say yes . . .
>
> If you write an article for a website and they love it, and you ask for pay for it, if you haven't published a book, chances are they'll say no.

But if you have published a book, chances are they'll say 'How much do you want?'"

Susan Campbell, author of *Getting Real: The Ten Truth Skills You Need to Live an Authentic Life*, echoes Jay's thoughts:

"Having a published book is like a 250 page business card. It gives people information about the kind of things you offer. When you write a book, you're writing to educate, but you're also writing to let people know how they can benefit by buying your product or using your service. There are numerous ways to integrate that kind of information into the book's message. Most of my income from the book comes, not from royalties, but from new clients who have come to me after reading my book."

Individual clients are only one way a book can add to your income.

Fred Gleeck, author of *Speaking for Millions*, says that a published book gives you a significant edge in getting speaking engagements, too. He says authors have three advantages over everyone else:

1) They earn more per speech than speakers without books.
2) They have an easier time getting radio and television interviews, which he says are "your best ticket to getting speaking engagements".
3) Organizations or associations see authors as a safer choice when hiring a speaker. "If there is a problem" Fred says, "the person who recommended you can always cover their rear end by saying that 'the guy had a book'."

In general, he says, "Your book becomes your single best piece of promotional material. The best example I can give you is one that I tell every time I give a speech to a group of speakers. I remember sitting next to a guy on an airplane. We got to talking. After I told him that I was a speaker and consultant, he asked me for a business card. I told him I didn't have a business card on me, but asked if he wanted a copy of my book. The look on his face was priceless. He was awestruck. People revere authors. Giving someone a copy of your book is the best promotional piece you can use to promote yourself."

Rich Fettke, author of *Extreme Success*, says a book makes a major difference in whether you are able to get the media exposure you want for your business:

"The media outlets that I'd tried to reach before, whether it was morning television, news shows, or print, [or] radio, all this, every time I'd contact a media outlet and try to set up an interview it was always 'who's your publisher?' The media outlets use publishers almost as a filter . . . Since June, when the book came out, I've done about 75 radio interviews, 15 television shows . . . *USA Today* and Dr. Laura."

What other opportunities can come your way from having a published book?

- Steven Mitchell Sack says that when he was promoting *The Working Woman's Legal Survival Guide,* "I was a guest on a radio show and the producers thought so highly of me they eventually hired me to conduct and host my own national show. I do *Jobs and Careers with Attorney Steve Sack* through the United Broadcasting Network, live every Sunday from 2 to 5. That was an outgrowth of my book work."[1]
- Frances Weaver was in her seventies when she wrote *The Girls With The Grandmother Faces.* After an interview on the *Today* show, they offered her an eighteen-month contract to appear on camera as the senior lifestyles editor.
- Jacqueline Marcell wrote *Elder Rage*, about coping as her father's caregiver when dementia caused him to become aggressive. She became an activist for eldercare reform and because of her book, she's been invited to testify before Congress. She has appeared on the cover of AARP Magazine, and on many radio and television shows including *Good Morning America.*

Marcell says publishing a book sets you apart. "Without the book, I would be somebody who was a caregiver and went and took care of her parents. Yeah, so? There are five million people with Alzheimer disease. How many people do you think there are who are caregivers? There are fifty million people that are caring for someone . . . A book is a vehicle to becoming the 'expert'."

MAGIC IN THE AIR

What is it about having a published book that leads to so many opportunities? Public relations people have a saying that "things lead to things".

Publishing a book involves a kind of alchemy. It takes an author's abstract thoughts and feelings and turns them into a tangible, recognizable "thing".

This tangible 'thing' has magic in it. First of all, it changes an author's status. Not many people succeed at turning their knowledge into something everyone can see. Maybe people are so impressed by authors because, in a sense, authors are shamans.

Once published, these shamans have additional credence as experts, which allows them easier access to publicity via newspapers, radio and television.

Some members of the audiences these media reach will be interested in what the authors know and will buy the book the author talked about.

Some of those who read it will form an almost magical bond with the author. Literary agent Jillian Manus explains it this way:

"Honor and trust the immense power of the written word. There is no more intimate connection than what exists between the eye and the

---

[1] From *You Can Make It Big Writing Books* by Jeff Herman

page. Nothing intervenes between the eye and brain. It is as if your words are little explosions in a reader's mind."

Those readers who are sympathetic to the author's ideas will ruminate on these concepts and how they relate to their own life or work.

They will feel a sense of trust and kinship with him. They will view the author as a benevolent advisor. Soon they will buy other things from him, or pay to see him at a seminar, or support causes he believes in, or just root for him to succeed at his endeavors. In short, in modern terminology, they are his fans.

You can accomplish a lot in this world if you have fans. They are a built in audience for anything you do.

And the more fans you have, the more good you can do. Just ask the Paul McCartneys and the Elizabeth Taylors of this world.

How soon would YOU like to have a base of fans that are ready to spend money on everything you do?

What could YOU accomplish if you had a published book?

How far would you go to make this happen ASAP? What if there was a shortcut you could take?

There is a shortcut. Hire a ghostwriter.

One Size Fits All

Honestly, everyone could benefit from the help of a ghostwriter. Here are four reasons why:

1) **Writing a book takes an enormous amount of time**. In this society, not only are we expected to be talented enough to do everything ourselves, we are also expected to find the time to do it.

   This is nuts! To find the hours to write a book, you have to sacrifice time at work, money (since you are working less), family time, and your social life. You do, however, enjoy an intimate, one on one relationship with your laptop. Is the ego gratification that comes from saying "I wrote every last word of this book myself" really worth it?

2) **Speed**. When do you want the benefits that come from a published book to accrue to you? The sooner the better. Using a ghostwriter is a shortcut to a published book—and to the quantum leap your business will take when you become an author.

3) **Your odds of getting published increase**. Two million manuscripts were submitted to publishers in 2002. Publishers purchased less than one percent of those. What percentage of the rejects do you think were ghostwritten? (My guess? Less than three percent.) Yet 50% of books that succeed with publishers are ghostwritten. Self-help guru Anthony Robbins says the best way to be successful at something is to copy the strategies of those who have already done it. Go with the odds. You are far more likely to get published with a ghostwriter than without one.

4) **Two heads are better than one**. The first time you undertake a project as daunting as a book, it makes sense to share the responsibility, especially if you can afford to hire someone with more experience than you have. Your ghostwriter may even be willing to supply personal anecdotes that relate to your topic.

Donald Bain, an author of over eighty books, most of which he ghostwrote (including a surprising amount of fiction), says that he made a conscious decision in this regard: "I was writing a book for a well-known person . . . I'd reached a point in the manuscript where an episode from my own life would fit perfectly. I paused. Should I waste it on someone else's behalf? My two 'rules' came into play: This is the most important thing I'll ever write, and it may be the last. I used my personal experience in the book, and have continued to do so throughout my ghostwriting career."

Here's an extra reason two heads are better than one: You can write the fun stuff and save the boring parts for your ghostwriter.

SPECIAL ORDERS

The next few reasons to hire a ghostwriter don't apply to everyone. If one or more applies to you, though, find a ghost to work with:

- You know enough to fill a book; you just don't like to write.
- You don't want to spend the time alone that writing a book requires.
- You're not quite sure how to turn what you know into a book.
- When it comes to writing, you aren't exactly Shakespeare.

WHEN TO FLY SOLO

It's a slight exaggeration to say that everyone should hire a ghostwriter. If there is no urgency for you to finish a book, if it won't help you build your business, if you have the time to write and you really enjoy it, go ahead, create a book on your own.

Though most people expect actors to use ghostwriters, Shirley MacLaine is an actress who has made a second career as a writer. She has written six books in her own inimitable voice, all without help.

Another actor, Michael J. Fox recently penned his memoirs, *Lucky Man*, for Hyperion Books. (He did. Oprah even said that when she was at his house, she saw him writing it.) Fox mentions that he always had an affinity for writing: "Even at five and six, I was writing long, multistanza, epic poems about my adventures, real and imagined, and later moved on to short stories, essays and reports that won praise."

Maybe you're like *them*.

Then again, neither of them had a day job when they were writing. Ms. MacLaine wrote her books between movies and Mr. Fox wrote his after he retired from the television show "Spin City".

But if a published book is a critical part of your business plan, find a ghostwriter to help you finish it quickly. Set aside your love for writing until you can afford the luxury of writing on your own.

Current And Potential Ghostwriters

If working with a ghostwriter *is* the path you want to take, there are several options to explore. You can hire someone who has ghostwritten previously, which can be expensive, or you can save money by working with a capable writer who doesn't have a book credit yet.

Before you decide, there's one piece of information you need: Most people don't write an entire manuscript before they land a book contract.

For non-fiction, you submit only a sample of the book: a detailed outline, two chapters, a biography and some pages about marketing. (Section II, *Land A Book Deal From Just Twenty Pages*, covers this in detail.) Book publishers and literary agents prefer this sample to a complete manuscript. If they like it, they will pay you to finish writing your book.

Knowing this may allow you to afford a more qualified writer than you previously thought was possible. You only need to be able afford enough to land a book contract—then, with the big publishers, your book advance will cover the rest of his fee.

I divide ghostwriters and potential ghostwriters into four categories based on success and experience. These classifications, from most expensive to free, are:

1) Unheralded Superstars
2) Established Ghostwriters
3) Quality Craftspeople
4) Future Experts

Unheralded Superstars are the folks behind bestsellers you have read. *Established Ghostwriters* are ghosts who have been published, but haven't made the top of the charts yet. *Quality Craftspeople* are talented professionals with writing, but not book experience. *Future Experts* are scribes who, up till now, haven't been paid to write, but have the talent and ability to put a book together.

In the next several chapters, each of these classes of writers will be examined in detail, starting with the most expensive. For each group, I'll cover the pros and cons, how much it costs to hire them (and why) and where you can find them.

CHAPTER 4

UNHERALDED SUPERSTARS

Most people think if you've done it once, you can do it again.

That's the main reason people hire an Unheralded Superstar to ghostwrite their books.

If you're a ghostwriter and your work appears on the *New York Times* bestseller list, you are one of a small group of people. Books that make the list ordinarily stay for a long time. Each week, only two or three new volumes make the cut, and often one of those is returning after dropping off. It's safe to say that there are less than a hundred bestselling non-fiction books each year.

If ghostwriters write half of all books, only fifty ghostwriters make this list each year. (Reach these heights a second time and you are part of an even smaller club, a Barry Bonds or Julia Roberts of ghostwriting.)

There are five good reasons to hire an Unheralded Superstar:

1) **An Unheralded Superstar's writing and research skill almost guarantees you a published book**. A writer of this caliber will only work with you if she thinks the idea for your book has appeal for a large audience. She also has great relationships with editors and agents who have profited from her bestselling books. Your book proposal will be an easy sell to these people.

2) **Your publisher is likely to give you a bigger book advance**. A book advance is money paid to the author before the book is published. When a bestselling ghostwriter is attached to a project, publishers have confidence that the finished product will be well written and on time. They will pay you more if they believe your book is a sure thing.

3) **Your publisher is likely to give your book an extra push.** Major publishers put out 150 or more books per season. Out of those books, only the top 20 or so get chosen for special treatment. If your book is not one of those books, the publisher just sends out review copies and a press release. But when your book is selected, it gets what Rick Horgan, Executive Editor of HarperCollins calls the Big Push:

   "Those books get a full-page ad in the *New York Times* . . .Those books will have radio spots . . . a publicity tour . . . [and] book club selections. They'll probably have a lot of money lavished on the cover . . . [and] counter displays; perhaps special discounts will be offered to get the book into the bookstores in quantity . . . The publisher pays a fee to get the book in the [chain] store window(s)."

4) **You have a significantly greater possibility of a bestseller.** See above.

5) **You will be able to tell all your friends that you are working with the same writer as** (fill in the blank with your favorite celebrity author).

There are *two negative factors*. First off, you need a lot of credibility in order for a writer of this status to agree to work with you. Unheralded Superstars only work with people who have the strongest credentials in their field. Secondly, these folks literally cost as much as a house—starting at $100,000 per book. Your initial investment in a book proposal could be $20,000. If you land a book contract, your whole book advance will go to publicity and your writer.

But if you are a big enough name in your field that just the fact that you are writing a book will be newsworthy, it makes sense to hire an Unheralded Superstar.

The reason is simple. It doesn't matter if you make money on the book A bestseller turns your name into a recognizable brand. When that happens, the money you make from speeches, videos, seminars, and consulting work is outrageous. Management guru Tom Peters earns $65,000 per speech.

In an article in *Inc.* magazine, an Unheralded Superstar anonymously explains why his business clients spend so much on him:

> "The smart 'authors' today view their books as loss leaders. I'm ghosting a book for which a major publisher gave the named author a $250,000 advance. After agent fees and expenses, I am getting the entire advance to create the book, which will be out this fall. Why would 'the author' readily give up a quarter of a million dollars (besides the fact that I am such a charmer)? The reason is simple. He figures his consulting business will go up $5 million a year once he has a book to leave behind on sales calls. 'Spending' $250,000 to generate $5 million is a 20:1 return."

PRICE EXPECTATIONS

The Unheralded Superstar quoted above says his minimum price is $200,000 for a complete book. He also receives a "hefty" portion of the royalties. It takes him four months to write a book.

His price for a book proposal? $25,000.

Wordworks is a bargain by comparison. This Boston company, comprised of nine journalists who have worked for prestigious publications like *Time*, *Newsweek*, and the *New York Times*, charges a over a hundred thousand dollars plus royalties to write your book. They are certainly worth it—they've hit the Times best-seller list numerous times with books like *Reengineering the Corporation* and authors like Tom Peters.

Georgetown University journalism professor and author Barbara Feinman, joined this club by writing the manuscript for *It Takes A Village*. Her contract with

Hillary Clinton called for payment of $120,000 and that she be mentioned in the acknowledgements section of the book. However, First Lady Clinton reneged. Feinman was only paid $90,000 and given no credit in the book.

Unfortunately, you won't be able to hire her to write a book with you. After nine books as a ghostwriter, including one with the Prince of Saudi Arabia, Feinman feared losing her own writing voice and has returned to her original passion—writing novels.

Few writers share the pedigree of an Unheralded Superstar. If you can even find one, you won't be in much of a bargaining position. You'll want her more than she wants you.

Expect to spend anywhere from $15,000 and $25,000 to hire an Unheralded Superstar to write your book proposal. The full book will cost you at least $100,000. Don't expect to haggle over her fee or her share of the royalties, as both will be set in stone. She won't give you a discount for putting her name on the cover of your book. Why should she stop writing anonymously? She makes too much money writing as a ghost.

FINDING UNHERALDED SUPERSTARS

How do authors meet ghostwriters who are this successful?

Frequently, an agent introduces them. Here's how Jeffrey Christian, author of *The Headhunter's Edge,* developed his book:

> "My PR man extraordinaire, Rob Wyse . . . introduced me to New York literary agent Jim Levine, who came up with the idea of the book I should write. Jim then connected me with the writer Edward Tivnan, who helped us fine-tune a proposal that sparked the interest of several publishing houses. I was delighted that Random House seemed as enthusiastic about the idea as we were. Over the next year, Tivnan helped me turn what I learned as a headhunter into a book that would help readers build their careers and their business."

Rick Wolff, Executive Editor for Warner Business Books, mentions three scenarios:

> "An author and a ghostwriter may come as a package deal. Sometimes a celebrity feels comfortable with an interviewer and they do the book together. Otherwise, I call writers I know. If they aren't available, I'll call a few agents."

If you want to find an Unheralded Superstar, you could call agents and editors and ask them to recommend someone. But since they don't know you, you might not be taken seriously. You might wind up with a recommendation—but instead of sending you to the accomplished writer you are looking for, they might just send you to somebody they owe a favor to.

The best way to convey how serious you are is to request someone specific. So you are going to have to do your homework.

Head to your bookstore with a pen and some paper. March to the section of the store where you hope your book will someday reside. Snatch all the bestsellers from this section and put them in a heap.

Examine the cover, the title page, and the acknowledgements of each book. If a second writer is listed somewhere, put the book in a pile to save. Remember, authors use a lot of euphemisms to describe ghostwriters, so if someone is thanked for their organizing skills, etc., trust your instincts. If you think they might be a ghostwriter, they probably are. (If you skipped 'Ghost Test Your Bookstore', see Chapter 2)

Skim through a few pages of each book in your saved pile to check for writing style. If a book's not written in a style you enjoy, eliminate it. Make note of any books you find particularly appealing.

Whatever books remain form the basis of your ghost search. Write down each book's title, author, and publisher. Include the co-author's name, if it's on the cover.

Next, go to the title page to write down what city the publisher is in. Then re-read the acknowledgements section in order to write down the names of the author's agent, ghostwriter, editor, and if possible, the editor's assistant.

Continue this process until you've made it through all the books in your pile.

If you want to try to contact these writers directly, your best bet is to go to your library's reference desk and ask for a copy of *Literary Market Place* (LMP). LMP is the yellow pages of the publishing business. If an Unheralded Superstar is listed anywhere, he's listed there.

While you're there, look up the publishers and agents on your list and write down their phone numbers. Keep this in a safe place, even if you find a ghostwriter without it. Since these agents and publishers are all work with books related to your topic, they are good targets for your book proposal.

If you found the writer's number, you can call him directly. Tell him that you are looking for a ghostwriter and you found his phone number in *Literary Marketplace*. Make sure you mention his book.

If that doesn't work, the next person to try is the author's agent. Now that you have a specific writer to ask for, your call is likely to be more successful.

I will e-mail you a list of over 400 agents and their contact information, including their websites, as a bonus for buying this book. The agent you are trying to reach is probably on this list. Send an e-mail with the subject "agents", followed by your first and last name, to: GetPublished@AuthorsTeam.com.

You can also find contact information for agents in a book called *Writer's Market* which is available at most bookstores. There is also an online version of this book at http://www.writersmarket.com. *Writer's Market* is discussed in greater detail in Chapter 6.

If you try all of these resources and you still can't find a particular agent's phone number, try to get this information from the book's publisher. Call the editor's assistant, if you know his name. If not, see if you can get the operator to tell you what it is. As a last resort, call the editor directly and hope that she will return your call.

Once you have a phone number, call the agent's office and ask, "Does your agency represent (name of the ghostwriter you would like to hire)?"

The person on the phone will answer one of two ways: "Yes" or "Why do you ask?"

In either case, say this: "I noticed she was involved in the book, _____. I have significant experience in _____, and I was hoping to discuss the possibility of hiring her to collaborate on a book proposal." (If you are a high level manager for a large corporation and you want to write a business book, mention your company's name and your title.)

Make sure you use the word "hiring" so it is clear that you understand that you will be paying for these services. Use the term "book proposal" to indicate you have at least a little knowledge of the book publishing world.

Hopefully, the agent or the agent's assistant will take you seriously and enter into further discussions with you. If not, mention your budget for a proposal and for the book. This will give you greater credibility.

If the agent's assistant will have the agent get back to you or the agent will present your basic idea to the Unheralded Superstar, consider this call a success.

In either case, set up an appropriate follow-up time, preferably within a week.

You eventually want to be asked to meet face to face with your ideal collaborator, so you can pitch your book directly to her. When you meet with her, hold her to the same standards you would any other writer. A detailed list of questions to ask is on page 49.

If you receive a negative response from the agent's office, such as "Mr. Unheralded Superstar is too busy writing a book on his own", it's best to move on to the next person on your list, or the next category if you're out of people.

Most ghostwriting owes more to technique than it does to talent. The difference between an Unheralded Superstar and a senior Established Ghostwriter has more to do with perception than actual skill. There's actually a certain amount of luck involved when it comes to making the bestseller list.

Just because an Unheralded Superstar has written bestsellers before, there is no guarantee he will make your book into one. Nor is there any reason to believe that your book won't make it to the top of the list if you hire an Established Ghostwriter.

Timing, luck, and how good a publicist you have are factors in determining whether your book becomes a bestseller. Taken together, they are more important than which ghostwriter helped write your book.

CHAPTER 5

ESTABLISHED GHOSTWRITERS

Established Ghostwriters are folks who write books for a living, sometimes even under their own name. The more books a ghost has written, the better, (and more expensive), it will be for you. If you can afford an Established Ghostwriter, it makes sense for you to hire one. Here's why:

1) The average book is about 80,000 words long. (400 words per page X 200 pages = 80,000.) Developing and sustaining 80,000 words on one subject takes a special kind of talent. Established Ghostwriters have a track record doing this.

2) You can safely assume that they will successfully create an entire book from your ideas. (Conversely, if you don't have enough material to fill a book, they will know quickly and you won't wind up wasting a lot of money.)

3) Established Ghostwriters give publishers (and you) confidence that your book will live up to professional standards and that it will be finished on time.

4) Established Ghostwriters have written book proposals that publishers have bought, making it more likely your book proposal will sell.

5) An Established Ghostwriter's relationships with editors and literary agents can make it easier for you to land a book contract.

6) You'll receive a larger advance for your book if editors think highly of the Established Ghostwriter who is writing with you. The larger your advance, the more marketing muscle your publisher will put behind your book.

The *disadvantages* of working with Established Ghostwriters are really a matter of degree. They cost more than Quality Craftspeople and they give your book less prestige than when you work with Unheralded Superstars. Less prestige might mean a lower advance and possibly, less of a publicity push from your publisher.

Of course, this might not matter. Since Established Ghostwriters cost significantly less than Unheralded Superstars, you could hire your own publicist with the money you save.

PRICE EXPECTATIONS

This category covers a wide range of writers. Some have written as many as fifty published works while others have just one or two under their belt. So prices vary tremendously.

Some Established Ghostwriters charge a flat fee of between $4000 and $10,000 for a book proposal.

Others charge an hourly rate, ranging from $40 to $125 per hour, according to the Editorial Freelancers Association. A book proposal takes around one hundred hours to write.

Their fee for a whole book runs between $30,000 and $75,000.

Many writers will charge half of the advance you receive from a publisher, as long as their share is no less than their minimum price.

But since the amount of work required for each book is different, most writers don't have a standard price.

Mark Steissel wrote *Guerilla Publicity* with Jay Conrad Levinson, Rick Frishman, and Jill Lublin. He has also ghosted many other books.

He says, "If I find a project that really interests me, I'm willing to be flexible on what I charge." He also said that if work is slow you might get a lower price out of him. You never know how lucky you could get.

When it comes to royalties, the top Established Ghostwriters expect a fifty-fifty split.

Less experienced writers will be more flexible and may be willing to give up some royalties for more money, or for credit on the book's cover or title page.

ONE MORE PIECE OF INFORMATION-- If the fees mentioned above sound expensive, here is some good news: An Established Ghostwriter knows how to write a proposal so that you will receive a larger advance than the typical first time author. So your book advance should at least cover her total cost, and possibly a great deal more.

How To Find Established Ghostwriters

If you are looking for an Established Ghostwriter who has worked on books in the same subject area as your book, follow the procedures outlined on page 19, with two differences: 1) Make sure you go to a chain bookstore like Border's or Barnes & Noble. This way you will be working with a writer who has had at least reasonable sales. 2) Instead of examining bestsellers, look at books that are less well known. *If you want someone with connections to agents and editors interested in your topic, this is a very good route.*

The American Society of Journalists and Authors, the nation's leading organization of over a thousand independent nonfiction writers, has a Writer Referral Service at (212) 398-1934, fax (973) 257-1851, or writers@asja.org. They charge $75 to $150 to help you find a writer, depending on how much they help with your search.

Enjoying this book? You can find me and my team at:
831-458-1550
GetPublished@AuthorsTeam.com
http://www.AuthorsTeam.com
We have a network that covers a wide variety of topics through the books we have written, the research for this book, our e-zine and through our teleseminars. We have a relationship with many agents and editors. Also, if you want to self-publish, we can get your book distributed to bookstores nationwide.

The Editorial Freelancers Association is a national, nonprofit, professional organization of self-employed workers in the publishing and communications industries. They have a job board where you can post your need for a ghostwriter at: http://www.the-efa.org/forms/jobphoneform.html

Search for Ghostwriters on the web. Go to http://www.google.com/advanced_search?hl=en, the advanced search version of Google. In the top box, insert "Ghostwriter" without the quotation marks. In the bottom box, "without the words", type "PBS", "TV", and "television" (without the quotes) to avoid the many sites associated with the children's television show *Ghostwriter*.

For freelance writers who have ghosted books on your topic: Try www.freelancewriters.com. You can pick writers by very specific topics here. For example, you can look for someone who has written about acupuncture, rather than just health.

Find Canadian writers and take advantage of the exchange rate by going to www.writers.ca.

Where to find bargains on the net: There are several sites where you can ask for bids from freelancers. I was surprised to find a number of traditionally published ghosts and authors bidding for work at very low prices, *between $3000 and $8000 to write an entire book!*

If you try one of these services, don't let yourself get overly impressed by a writer's credentials. It's the writing samples that count. At least half of the samples I received from previously published scribes were below the standards I expect from the writers I hire.

If you choose to work with one of these writers, make sure you check his references. In particular, ask his editors how much editing they had to do to the final draft in order to come up with the finished product. Otherwise, you might hire a mediocre writer with a very talented editor. Also, get info on how timely he was in handing in his manuscripts or articles.

Here are some of the sites where you can get bids for your project:

> www.creativemoonlighters.com
> www.prosavvy.net
> www.elance.com

Be careful, though. I've heard success and disaster stories from people who've hired writers this way.

CHAPTER 6

WHO CAN WRITE YOUR BOOK FOR LESS?
QUALITY CRAFTSPEOPLE!

When I was a headhunter, I worked with a number of start-ups on shoestring budgets. Occasionally, they would ask me to help them find an employee with special talents; one who could move the sun, the stars and the and the skies, in order to get their product out the door.

Then they would tell me the salary range.

Sometimes I had to bite my lip to keep from laughing.

Their budget was completely out of whack. They simply couldn't afford to hire someone with the experience they wanted.

After carefully and gently explaining this, I would ask," What do you really need to do this project? Is there someone who can get most of the job done? If necessary, can we bring in a consultant for the trickier stuff?"

There was always someone who fit the bill. Maybe not someone with an industry-wide reputation, but someone who could do the job. An additional consultant was rarely needed.

Those are the same questions I asked myself before I wrote the next few chapters. Who has the talent and experience to write a book even if they haven't written one before?

There are several answers. Here is a list, in order of preference:

1) Magazine editors and the writers who work for them
2) Freelance writers
3) Amateurs with great portfolios (People who have written great web pages, reporters for college newspapers, and members of a fiction or non-fiction writing group.)
4) People who write lyrics or poetry

FINDING BARGAIN BASEMENT WRITERS

You can't call just any magazine editor or writer and expect them to write for you at a bargain price. Folks who work for *Sports Illustrated, Fortune, Time*, and other national publications with millions of readers, are offered as much as the top Established Ghostwriters when they collaborate on a book.

Not to sound like a mercenary, but you are looking for a writer or an editor who is currently paid sweatshop wages.

Lucky for you, there are plenty of gifted people like that.

Since the number of people who want to be writers and editors far exceeds the total number of available jobs, hordes of people with degrees in English and journalism are barely scraping by.

Or they earn a little extra with their writing while they work at something else.

Or they write epic web pages as a hobby.

That leaves many low-income journalists happy to have a job at all.

That's who you want for your book. Here's why:

- They're likely to take on extra work to boost their income.
- Since they're used to getting paid poorly, they'll have lower expectations in terms of what you will pay them.

QUID PRO QUO

Before you feel like a crass opportunist, let me say that you bring one thing to the table that is far more valuable than money to an unpublished writer.

You bring something to write about.

Not that most writers run out of ideas. It's just that to get a book published on a particular subject, you need to be a credible expert.

The one subject professional writers are credible experts on is how to write. Publishers are saturated with books on that topic.

The majority of books are about doing—either how to do something (how-to, business and cookbooks), or what people have done (history), or what one person did (biography and autobiography), or a commentary about things people do today (pop culture).

YOU do or have done something. Allowing a writer to write about that with you is a great gift to him.

Your credibility gives a collaborator a greater chance of getting published. Your far-reaching experience in your field is what publishers are looking for.

Peter Rubie, a former editor who is currently both a literary agent and a writer, explains it this way:

> "You need to have some sort of credentials to write nonfiction. A parish priest could write a major work on religion and get it published; a teacher could write a book about education . . . You need to have some edge, however small, beyond your interest in the topic, though."[2]

Experience is a primary factor when Bantam executive editor Toni Burbank selects a book:

> "What really turns me on is that the author has in some way been preparing all of his or her life to write this book. There is a tremendous commitment on the author's part to this work. That commitment will evoke a mirroring commitment in me. That's publishing at its best."[3]

---

[2] From his book, *The Everything Get Published Book*
[3] From *Book Editors Talk to Writers,* by Judy Mandell

EASY BAKE BOOKS

Here's another benefit to the writer: It's faster writing a book with you than without you.

How is this possible?

When writers want to create non-fiction books on topics they aren't experts on, they turn to history, biographies, or pop culture commentaries. Each of these categories requires time-consuming research and interviews.

On the other hand, ghostwriters gather information much more quickly by interviewing the author they are writing with. As British ghostwriter Andrew Crofts' blithely explains it:

> "By using someone else's knowledge I can cut my research time for a book from months to days because I'm going straight to the source of the material rather than having to ferret around in cuttings libraries and drink endless cups of tea in the front rooms of the subject's childhood friends and relatives."

CLIMBING THE LADDER

Ghostwriting a book is a very strong career move for your collaborator. Getting published will change his professional life in a variety of ways. A book in print gives him the experience to charge at least $40 per hour for ghostwriting, even more if your book becomes well known. He has a piece of work that he can put in the hands of agents and publishers. They can give him additional opportunities to write more books, after which he can charge even more money. He will also develop a relationship with at least one editor (more if your book receives multiple offers) and one agent, which will prove quite useful when he inevitably wants to pitch a book idea of his own.

The late author and ghostwriter Gary Provost used to compare the obstacles freelance writers face to the difficulties one would have getting into an upside down pyramid. "The toughest trick is getting in that little pinpoint at the bottom with your first story, first book, first anything. Once you get in, you can start to throw your weight around and make room for yourself . . . the higher you rise, the easier it is."

You can help a writer enter that pyramid. And to a writer, that is a benefit significantly more valuable than money.

CHAPTER 7

MAGAZINE EDITORS

It's time to find someone you can write with.

Your best alternative, in the universe of people without a published book, is a magazine editor.

Editors have four things going for them: They are responsible for making sure the articles in their magazine are well written and enjoyable to read.

1) They are likely to have a pleasant writing style and you won't have to worry about any grammar mistakes.
2) They are experts at meeting deadlines.
3) As editors, they are used to looking for stories with unusual slants. That will be useful, since you will want to give your book an interesting angle that distinguishes it from other books on the same topic.
4) They understand how to write with a particular audience in mind.
5) They are also a good source of referrals. If they can't work with you, they will know salaried and freelance writers you should talk to about becoming your ghostwriter.

There are two areas where magazine editors might fall short.

1) They've never written a full-length book
2) They might not know anything about writing a book proposal.

Fortunately, both these skills can be easily picked up.

Here's a strategy to help you find an editor who will cost less than an Established Ghostwriter. First of all, the ideal candidate will work for a small publication with a circulation of less than 100,000.

Even in periodicals that small, certain editors are better compensated than others. To find editors in the right salary range, you need to know something about the organizational chart at magazines.

A SHORT TUTORIAL ON EDITORIAL HIERARCHY

The person running the show at a magazine is called the editorial director, the editor-in-chief, or at a small periodical, the editor.

Next down the ladder is the senior editor.

That's not a typo. In the magazine business, senior editors report to a boss with the plain old vanilla title of editor.

Quirky, huh?

A senior editor is a writer who's worked at a magazine for a long time. He writes feature articles and contributes to the overall editorial vision of the magazine.

Below a senior editor is the managing editor.

The managing editor is a reporter who was promoted. She manages all the details of getting a magazine finished on time. She also oversees copy editors and writes photo captions.

Folio, a periodical about magazine management, did a salary survey in May of 2002. They detailed the average salary for editors of publications with fewer than 100,000 readers. Here are the averages for each title:

Editorial Director or Editor-In-Chief	$76,539
Editor or Executive Editor	$60,939
Managing Editor	$49,974
Senior Editor	$53,337

A statistic from the Department of Labor shows that half of the magazine editors in the United States earn even less. In the year 2000, according to the *Bureau of Labor Statistics Occupational Handbook 2002 – 2003*, the median annual earning for an editor of periodicals was $42,560.

That works out to $21.28 per hour when you divide it by the 2000 hours most full-time employees work during a year.

Since this is the median, then half of the editors of periodicals in the U.S. earn *less than that*.

These are the editors that we want to approach.

THE MAGAZINE EDITORS BARGAIN BIN

Where do you find an editor who earns less than the averages mentioned above?

- Magazines with lower circulations.
- Trade magazines. *Folio*'s survey shows "editors with less than five years of experience make substantially more at consumer titles."
- Magazines that come out less than once a month.
- Magazines whose main office is in a low cost area of the country.
- Magazines that pay freelancers less than fifty cents a word, or if they pay a flat rate, under $750 per article. If they are this thrifty with their writers, you can be sure the editor is treated the same way.

Writer's Market, mentioned previously, is a book that will enable you to search for magazines that meet most of these criteria. Their website, at http://www.writersmarket.com, is an even better solution if you want to find a writer who lives in your area.

Writer's Market is an eleven hundred page tome that provides a list of more than eight thousand book and magazine editors. It gives detailed information on more than a thousand publishers. Each magazine listing includes the magazine's circulation, how often it comes out, and what it pays. Writer's Market also breaks periodicals into two sections: consumer and trade (business to business) magazines.

The least expensive way to recruit an editor to write with you is to subscribe to the online version of *Writer's Market*. At press time, the cost for this was $2.99 per month for a monthly subscription, or $29.99 with a one-time annual payment. The online version is also the only way to search for magazines by location.

If you want to buy a printed version, the book is available for $29.99. Another version of this book, called *Writer's Market Online* includes access to the website for $49.99.

Price Expectations

As mentioned above, the going rate for an Established Ghostwriter is a minimum of $40 per hour, or about $4000 (100 hours) for a book proposal.

For the magazine editors we have been speaking of, a fair price for a book proposal would be $1500 to $2000. The idea is to convince the editor to let you pay him the same rate the magazine does.

That rate is likely to be less than $21 per hour since the targeted magazines are those that offer less than median pay. (As previously stated, the editors at these magazines earn $42,000 per year or less. Human resources professionals state a year's worth of work is 2000 hours, hence the figure of $21 per hour.)

If you can't afford $2100, sell the idea that ghosting a book is a great career move. (Review the section titled Quid Pro Quo on p. 25.) If you are persuasive, you might be able to talk an editor into working on your book proposal for a bit less. Here are some other strategies to use:

1) Convince the editor that: a) there is a wide audience for this book b) you are a credible expert on its subject matter and c) there is a logical reason to believe that you will be able to garner publicity for it. If the editor believes your book is a surefire winner, it will be easy for her to get on board no matter what you pay.

2) Tell the editor that when you land a book contract, if the advance is $30,000 or less you will give her as much as 70%. (If it is more than that, pay her either 50% or the $21,000 she would have earned under the $30K advance, whichever is higher.) Agree to split everything else evenly, including royalties. (The editor will be spending an enormous amount of time writing the book if you sell it. And she may be working for less than she is worth during the proposal phase, so reward her properly if the book sells.)

3) Since you will be paying her less money for the proposal, offer her more credit. Make the editor a co-author instead of a ghostwriter.

If you meet some of these conditions, there is a chance you'll be able to hire an editor to collaborate on your book proposal for less than $1500. And if she really believes in what you're working on, or if you are lucky enough to be working on a subject she is passionate about, she might even do it for free.

NARROWING YOUR SEARCH FOR AN EDITOR

We are seeking magazines that meet three basic criteria:

1) Do they have a circulation of less than 100,000?
2) Do they pay freelancers on the low end of the scale?
3) Do they come out less than once a month?

If you can answer yes to at least two of these questions, put the magazine's editor on your contact list.

A nationwide search will yield too many editors who fit these criteria. Narrow your search by looking for someone who lives in your area. Or, to increase your chance of finding the least expensive editor possible, search for someone who lives in an area with a very low cost of living.

The benefit of someone local, of course, is that you get to meet him in person. That can be beneficial in terms of building trust. And many people do their best work face to face.

For others, though, it may not be the most efficient way to collaborate.

I'm writing *Inside Out Weddings (and Other Soul Satisfying Ceremonies)* with a local minister. We find that working over the phone saves a tremendous amount of time. Not only do I save the forty minutes I used to spend driving to and from her house; we also seem to get down to business faster. The actual exchange of information seems more efficient, too.

With today's technologies, it doesn't matter whether you write with someone in a neighboring town or on the opposite side of the country.

You can use this to your advantage if you to minimize the costs. Look for a collaborator who lives in an area with a low cost of living. People in these locations are paid less than their counterparts in higher priced regions. And the less an editor earns at his magazine, the less he will expect you to pay him to write your book.

Need help finding these low cost areas? According to ACCRA, (formerly known as the American Chamber of Commerce Research Association) the least expensive state to live in is Arizona, followed by Tennessee, North Dakota and Alabama. You can find a list of the 20 least expensive cities at: http://tinyurl.com/5w97

SEARCHING WRITER'S MARKET

Please note: Follow these instructions even if you can't afford to hire an editor. Calling magazine editors is an excellent way to get referrals for freelance writers, who can be significantly less expensive than editors.

As mentioned earlier, Writer's Market Online is the best place to search for magazine editors who meet the criteria we are using.

So go to http://www.writersmarket.com.

Log in. (If you haven't yet subscribed, follow the instructions for subscribing.) On the left hand side of the page you will see white print on a black background. Click on the second entry, which says "Search Markets".

This takes you to a page with twelve yellow bars, each with the name of a market. The second one down on the left is "Consumer Magazines"; the second one down on the right says "Trade". Click on "Trade Magazines" first; they pay editors and writers less than consumer magazines.

The screen that will appear is a search form. Type the area code of the region you have selected as your target in the fourth box on the left hand side. (If you have chosen to search an entire state, click the arrow of the box next to the word "location", which is the third word down on the left.) When you click on the arrow, a list of abbreviations of states appears. Click on the bottom arrow until the abbreviation for your target state appears, then click on that abbreviation. It will now inhabit the box next to the word "location".) Then page down and click on the yellow bar that says "SEARCH WRITER'S MARKET".

A list will appear of trade magazines in your selected area. If you live in a region with lots of magazines, like Manhattan, you will need to eliminate the ones that are outside of the target group.

The easiest way to do this quickly is by looking at the number of dollar signs next to a magazine's name. This is the way that Writer's Market codes pay rates for freelance writers. Next to each magazine's name, there is a rating of between one and four dollar signs ($). The higher the pay, the more dollar signs a periodical receives.

If you want to save time, only click on those magazines with one or two dollar signs. (Our criterion for freelance pay matches the two dollar sign exactly.) These magazines usually either have circulations of less than 100,000 or come out less than once a month.

Select a magazine from your results and click on it. A web page about that magazine will appear. The name of the magazine and its address appears at the top on the left hand side. The phone number and the URL, if it has one, will be on the top right.

An inch or two down is a black bar. Two lines above it will be the word "contact"; underneath that will be the name of an editor and her exact title. This is the person you may want to recruit.

If another editor, say an editor-in-chief, runs the magazine, her title and name will appear above the word "contact".

On the first black bar are the words "About" and the title of the magazine.

Below it is a one-sentence description of the magazine. The word "Frequency" usually appears below that. Most magazines are described as "monthly", "bi-monthly" or "quarterly". Bi-monthly means every two months; quarterly means every three months.

The next black bar is titled "Freelance Facts". Under that will be some information in a box. The second line in that box frequently reveals the magazine's circulation.

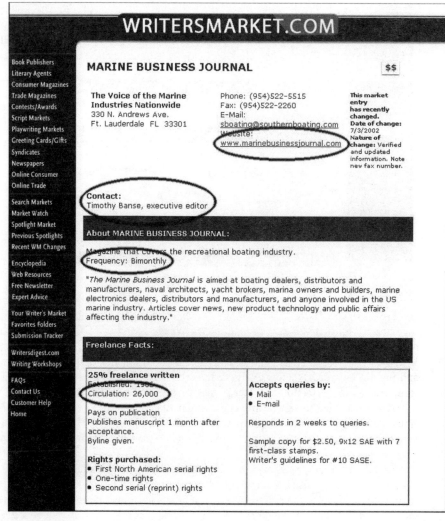

You now have the information you need to decide whether the editor of this magazine is a potential collaborator. If he is, look at the whole entry. The editor probably wrote the paragraph titled "Tips". Now scroll to the top of the page. If there is an URL (website) listed, click on it. This links you to the magazine.

The main page of a magazine typically lists a number of articles that appear in the current issue. Unfortunately, you probably won't get a chance to look at a column by the editor. Those columns usually aren't on the website. But you can look at the articles he has selected for his magazine.

Though it's hard to judge an editor's writing skills from that, you can tell if the stories look like they have appealing angles. If you were interested in the subject matter of this magazine, would you enjoy these articles?

Unless your answer is no, continue to consider this editor as a possible collaborator.

Scroll down to the next black bar below the one that says "TIPS". This is where you save shortcuts to the magazines you are interested in. Create a new folder, by typing in a name, like "Possible Ghosts", in the blank box next to the words "Create a new folder for _____". Then click on the yellow button that says "CREATE".

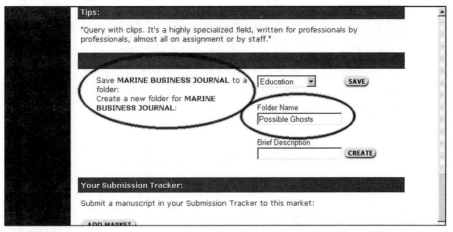

From now on, if you want to find this magazine, look at the black side bar and page down. "Favorite Folders" is under "My Writer's Market". Click on "Favorite Folders" and a list of your folders will appear with little blue boxes next to them. Ignore the blue boxes unless you want to delete a folder. Click on the blue ink spelling out the folder's name and your list of magazines will appear. You can then click on each magazine in the folder if you want to contact its editor.

When you want to save another magazine, all you have to do is go to the same black bar and click on the yellow button below it that says "SAVE". If you create more than one folder, make sure you are saving the magazine to the folder you want it in.

With luck, when you complete this process, you will have a number of trade magazines to choose from. On the other hand, there may not be any business-to-business magazines in your selected area. (Arizona has only one listing in the entire state.) Either way, check the consumer magazines.

Go back to the black bar on the left-hand side of the page. Click on "consumer magazines", insert the area code for the region you have selected, or pick the state and highlight it next to the word "location". Then click on the yellow bar that says "Search Writer's Market".

In other words, rinse, lather and repeat.

After running the consumer magazine search, if you haven't found enough people to choose from, use area codes from adjacent regions. Or search an entire state, either the one you live in or one with a low cost of living. If the state you select doesn't have enough choices, pick another one.

If you're still unhappy with your results, there's probably a weekly newspaper where you live. Its editor might be a good choice. You can also call the editors of free monthly magazines that you see at bookstores, coffee houses and restaurants.

HELPFUL HINTS

Don't pick the editor of a periodical whose subject is the same as your book. This editor is an expert at what his magazine is about, so he can charge more for writing on that subject.

If the pay rate for a magazine is in the two-dollar sign ($$) range, even if it doesn't meet the other criteria, try your luck. You never know how an editor is going to respond.

If possible, take a look at the magazine before you call the editor. Check your newsstand or your local bookstore. Or stop by the magazine's office for a copy. Or call and request that a copy be sent to you. (Depending on the magazine, this could take a long time.)

Usually, there is a note from the editor at the beginning of the magazine. Read this to get a taste of the editor's writing style. If you like it, give the editor a call.

CHAPTER 8

FREELANCE WRITERS

If you can't afford an editor or if you just can't find one, a freelance writer will do just fine. (Since most salaried writers moonlight as freelancers, we are lumping them together with this group.)

There are other advantages, besides cost, when you hire a freelance writer:

1) Unless he is extremely successful, a freelance writer has more time available for your project than an editor does, so your project may get finished more quickly.
2) He has a wider range of contacts because he works for a number of periodicals, so when your book gets published, he may be able to help you promote it.
3) The good ones write more than editors do, so they probably write faster.
4) Whereas an editor comes up with a variety of angles on one topic (i.e. bird watching, gardening, bodybuilding, etc.), a freelance writer comes up with story ideas for a variety of topics. So she may have more ideas for you than an editor would.
5) You can get recommendations for freelance writers from editors. It's always better to hire people that come highly recommended.
6) There are more freelance writers than editors, so you will have more people to choose from.

There are two potential drawbacks:

Any editor you speak with will have a verifiable track record of producing a certain amount of work on time. Since a freelance writer doesn't report to anyone, if she had a hit or miss history, you wouldn't find out about it.

When a freelance writer shows you her articles, someone else has edited her work. You can't be absolutely sure that the quality you see is the quality you'll get. (On the other hand, if an editor has recommended her, she probably submits work that is close to what is published. Editors prefer working with writers who submit work that doesn't take much editing.)

WHAT FREELANCERS EARN

To understand freelance writers and what they get paid, you need an idea of how much they write. Here's what the National Writer's Union says about the average fulltime freelancer's output:

"Freelance writers spend a tremendous amount of time looking for work (researching and pitching articles) and revising. While some articles can be done in a week, others may take three months. For most full-time freelance writers, selling and writing 3000 or 4000 words a month is about the best that they can expect to do – two feature articles or the equivalent in smaller pieces."

The pay a freelance writer receives can be mortifyingly low.

In *Writer's Market*, the publications that receive 2 dollar signs ($$) pay between ten and forty-nine cents a word. Or if they pay by the article, they pay between $150 and $750. Magazines that receive one dollar sign ($) pay less than that. Even the New York Times, arguably the most esteemed newspaper in America, pays freelancers as little as thirty cents per word. (They also pay as much as one dollar a word.)

With numbers like those, it shouldn't come as a surprise that in a survey by Content Exchange in July of 2000, 46% of all freelancers estimated that they would earn less than $20,000 that year from their writing. Of those who write full time, 25% expected to earn less than that.

Even more shocking is a survey from 1995 by the National Writers Union. They found that only 16% freelance writers earned more than $30,000.

These figures may explain why one part-time freelance writer, seemed so optimistic in a recent issue of WritersWeekly.com: "All totaled in the past 10 months, 11 of my stories have appeared . . . The pay has been okay, too. One of the publications only pays about $75 per story, another pays about $100 for a story, the third one pays 40 cents a word, and one pays considerably more . . . I'm not making a living off my writing, not even close, but for me this is a success story."

PRICE EXPECTATIONS

What do these figures mean to you?

They mean that, no matter what your budget, there is someone who has been paid to write that you can afford to hire.

A writer like the one quoted above is certainly going to find the idea of $1000 to write a twenty-five to forty page book proposal appealing.

He may even be happy with $500, if it means a chance to be paid to collaborate on the book if it sells.

And you might be able to get him to write a proposal for free, if he believes your book will sell. I have a feeling he won't be as jaded or picky as a magazine editor.

I am not advocating that you take advantage of poorly paid writers. A writer should be paid a fair wage. Also, hire the best writer you can afford. This increases the likelihood that your book will be published.

However, if you can't afford to spend much of your own money, a writer like the one quoted above will do just fine.

FINDING FREELANCE WRITERS

As a headhunter, there were two ways I found people. One way was indirect; I would ask, for example, opto-mechanical engineers and their managers for names of other good opto-mechanical engineers they knew. Then I would call them. The other way was much more direct; instead of asking for referrals, I would ask those same opto-mechanical engineers if they would be open to a new opportunity.

The engineers I called directly never did as well on interviews as the ones that were referred to me by others. The people who gave me referrals acted like filters—they recommended gifted engineers and kept me from recruiting folks who weren't as skilled. On the other hand, when I called someone directly, I only knew how good he said he was. And believe me, there were plenty of engineers who had inflated ideas of their own ability.

That's why I can tell you with certainty that the best way to find a freelance or salaried writer is through an editor who has worked with her.

An editor knows each writer's strengths and weaknesses: who meets deadlines and who sees them as elastic; who submits perfect copy and who needs editing; who follows directions well, and who is inclined to "reinterpret" them.

There's also the subtle aspect of personality. You will be working closely with a ghostwriter for at least six months, if you land a book contract. You want to hire someone who is easy to get along with.

An editor will have a sense of writers and their personalities, too.

These are important considerations when you hire a writer.

In case you're wondering, it is much more difficult to find these kinds of things out about editors. However, the mere fact that editors run a magazine says they can meet deadlines and edit copy—which would suggest that they can edit their own copy, too. (It is a good idea, though, to check references on anyone you are going to hire.)

One of the best ways to find freelance writers who will work within your budget is to call the editors of magazines we mentioned above.

You may be calling these editors anyway, because you are trying to recruit them. If they will consider working with you, don't ask for referrals. However, if an editor lets you know he has no interest in collaborating, it would be appropriate to ask if he knows a few good writers you can approach.

If he gives you more than two names, ask him who he would call first, and why. Then ask who he would call second, etc.

If it is unlikely that you can afford to hire an editor as your ghostwriter, then you will have to take a slightly different approach. Just call the editor, explain a little about your project and your budget, and then ask her for referrals. Follow the script in the Appendix to this book.

If there are magazines in your selected area with a circulation of over 100,000 or that pay writers decent money, (those listed with three or more dollar signs ($$$) in *Writer's Market*), you can call them as well, though you may have a harder time reaching these editors directly. If the writers they recommend are too expensive, ask who they know.

If you live in an area where no magazines are published and you really want to work with someone you can meet with face to face, don't worry. As mentioned above, call the editor of your local weekly. He uses freelance writers. You can also try the editor of your local daily newspaper. (If that doesn't work for some reason, many newspapers list the e-mail addresses of their writers. You can e-mail one of them directly.)

How To Avoid Cold Calls

If you don't relish the idea of phoning total strangers, here are some ways to advertise directly to an audience of writers who may be open to the kind of money we have spoken about:

As mentioned previously, there are a number of sites where you solicit bids from freelance writers. Make sure you check references thoroughly before you hire anyone. See page 24 for the questions to ask. These sites are at:

www.creativemoonlighters.com
www.prosavvy.net
www.elance.com

Place a free ad in WRITERSWEEKLY.COM. WritersWeekly.com is an e-zine (that's a newsletter delivered by e-mail) distributed for free to 67,000 writers from all over the world. Here's their blurb:

"HAVE A NEED FOR CREATIVE FREELANCERS?
No charge to list it here! E-mail your 6-8 line employment ad with freelance pay rates to: writersweekly@writersweekly.com
No commission-based, no non-paying, no questionable payment terms. We only post legitimate, paying jobs for freelancers, and we post them at no cost."

The Work for Writers mailing list is an ongoing e-mail discussion group which professional writers use to find job leads, share information on job searches, writing contacts, contracts, writers' organizations, etc. The list also posts jobs from employers. You must subscribe to it to post a job. Subscribe by sending an e-mail to:
WorkForWriters-subscribe@yahoogroups.com.

Reply to the e-mail they send back to you in order to officially join. After that, you can send messages to the list by e-mailing WorkForWriters@yahoogroups.com .

There are advantages and disadvantages to advertising for a collaborator. On the positive side, you don't have to call anyone. No need to fear rejection. You write something, send it off, and if someone is interested, they contact you. And the pool of potential applicants can be quite large.

These are the negatives:

1) You could wind up with a huge number of applicants and feel overwhelmed with e-mails. Picture the judge's bench in *Miracle on 34th Street* after the postal workers dump all the sacks of mail addressed to Santa Claus on it.
2) When it comes to "glamour" jobs, and writing is one of them, you are more likely to run into someone who can't take no for an answer. This person will hound you for a job, even after you have filled the position.
3) Though folks who apply on their own are often very talented, you have a better chance of recruiting a high quality candidate through a referral.

Referrals are always more reliable than reference checks. After all, no one wants to stop someone she has employed from getting another job (unless she was horrible to work with).

When you advertise, if you want a collaborator who lives nearby, make sure you mention this—and use the word "only". Otherwise you will receive dozens of e-mails trying to persuade you to consider a long-distance writing relationship. (You will, of course, still get a few e-mails like this, but at least you won't get as many.)

Here's a sample ad:

Ghostwriter wanted for self-help book. $1000 fee for proposal. More generous terms for writing the rest of the book if accepted for publication. Only apply if you live in Silicon Valley area. Send 3 writing samples and a resume (formal or informal) to you@email.com.

CHAPTER 9

FUTURE EXPERTS:
IF YOU CAN'T AFFORD A PRO,
THERE'S STILL HOPE

If your book proposal budget is less than $500, you might strike out with freelance writers. But don't worry. There is still hope. Anyone with a little bit of writing talent can write a non-fiction book.

How do I know? Because I wrote my first book *without any writing experience.*

I had no published articles. No background in the subject matter. No multi-layered web page that showed I could write book-length material.

The writing sample that won me a shot at the job was short--a three page sales letter.

And the editor for a major New York publisher hired me on the basis of a single chapter.

Here's the full story:

In 1984, I was unsuccessfully attempting to write a Broadway musical (lyrics and music only— I will admit that I had a talent with words— but not much to show I could write prose.) I earned my keep doing telephone surveys for a direct marketing company, the Stenrich Group.

After indicating to a number of people that I was interested in learning to write ad and catalog copy, Richard, a salesman for the company, asked me to help him out. He was moonlighting as a consultant for two brothers who owned a beauty salon. Vincent and Fred Nardi had written a book, *Cut Your Hair Like a Pro.* Putnam Books, their publisher, was interested in a sequel about hair color.

They needed an outline to present to their editor.

Richard had been asked to make this happen.

He asked me if I could put one together. "By *tomorrow*," he said.

If I did a good job I might have a chance to ghostwrite the whole book.

"Sure," I answered. I may not have known much about hair color, but I understood what to do when opportunity knocked.

Armed with the outlines of *Cut Your Hair Like A Pro* and a recently published book on hair color, I went home.

I spent a lot of hours trying to pull a rabbit out of a hat that night. I didn't know anything about hair color. I didn't have enough writing experience to be aware that, no matter how ignorant I was of the subject matter, I could produce something publishable. But somehow, by 3 A.M., I had created the framework for a book.

When the editor accepted my outline, she agreed to look at a writing sample. My three page sales letter was all I had, so that was what I used. She ran it by a few other editors. (The large publishing houses do everything by committee.) They agreed I had enough ability for them to let me write a test chapter. Adrienne Ingrum, my editor, liked the chapter enough to entrust me with the rest of the book.

If a major Putnam was willing to let a completely untested writer compose a sample chapter, and from just that chapter hire him to write a book, then it's safe for you to do the same thing.

WEB PAGE WRITERS

There are a number of ways to find talented people who write well without getting paid. One possibility is to look for people who have written lengthy web pages.

There are a number of positives about this group:

1) You can see their work before you call them.
2) They love to write and are motivated. They've gone to the trouble to putting together a web page just for their musings. They obviously write just for the sake of writing.
3) They are already writing for free, so they might not charge you anything until you land a book contract.
4) If you pick the author of a lengthy site, you have evidence that she can produce a book's worth of material.
5) A lengthy site also indicates its author probably has the time to work on your project.
6) An additional benefit: this is someone who is capable of developing a website for your book.

There are also some drawbacks to hiring someone through a web page. Though you know the author of the page is motivated when she does her own work, you don't know what she is like when she works for someone else. You won't have a sense of whether she can meet deadlines or how good she is at following directions. She won't have proven experience trying to develop an angle for a story. And, as with all the groups mentioned above (with the exception of published ghostwriters), she is unlikely to know anything about writing a book proposal.

Then again, many of these issues can be addressed through interviews and reference checks. Most people have to follow directions, produce for others, and meet deadlines at their regular jobs. And folks who are avid readers of magazines and non-fiction quite often have unconsciously absorbed techniques for telling a non-fiction story and coming up with the right angle for a book.

PRICE EXPECTATIONS

Chris, a friend of mine, is a devoted fan of Japanese animation. This technique, called anime, is used on television shows such as Pokemon and Sailor Moon. It employs more color and faster movement than traditional animation. Unfortunately, a number of children in Japan have fainted or had epileptic attacks from watching anime, so creators have had to slow their work down.

In Japan, adults view these shows with their children, which feature sexuality, nudity, and violence that would not be culturally acceptable in the U.S. When the shows air here, the offending scenes are either airbrushed or edited out.

Chris has a website about *Dragon Ball Z*, his favorite anime show. It includes a collection of 14 essays criticizing the Americanization of a classic Japanese anime series. These editorials run between 2000 and 3000 words apiece.

Chris has also written an episode-by-episode guide that details the differences between the Japanese and the American versions of the show. Each article is between 500 and 2000 words long.

All told, Chris's labor of love adds up to well over 75,000 words. That is the size of at least a two hundred page book.

Not only is the sheer volume of his web site impressive, the quality of Chris's writing stands out, too. This site is so good that an editor at *Anime Invasion* called and asked Chris to write an article about *Dragon Ball Z* for his magazine. Anime Invasion is the leading magazine on the subject of Japanese animation and has 75,000 readers.

(By the way, to continue to hammer home the point that many freelance magazine writers get paid next to nothing, Chris wrote two thousand words and was paid three hundred dollars, or 15 cents per word.)

Though Chris has been paid to write, he doesn't consider himself a freelance writer yet. If someone approached him, he would be willing to write a book proposal for free.

> "I would do it for the experience. That would be my first exposure to the book publishing industry and it's a good way to get my feet wet. I'd be willing to do it as ghost. I would take a percentage of the advance, and ten percent of the royalties."

Since most web page writers work for free, it is no great leap to suppose that you can find one who will write your book proposal on spec for the chance to write a published book. If he wants to get paid, you will only need to pay him an honorarium-- something on the order of one hundred to two hundred and fifty dollars. Since this is probably the first time he will be paid to write, it doesn't make sense to pay him more than five hundred dollars.

Also, since he is so inexperienced, you will be able to keep a greater percentage of the book advance and the royalties than you could if you hired a professional writer. (Negotiating those aspects of your contract will be discussed later.)

ONE THING TO WATCH FOR: Some great web pages are by people who write professionally in the business world. They will not work for free. Check to see if the author of your favorite web page lists their occupation before you contact him.

FINDING TALENT ON THE WEB

Looking for talent on the web is a bit more time consuming than other approaches because you have to look at each web site you find to see if you like it.

You stand a better chance of locating a good writer if you are willing to work at a distance; some of the best pages on the web give no indication as to where the writer lives.

Here's a trick that will lead you to long, well-written web pages:

Look for fan pages.

Fan pages are electronic altars to the subject of a fan's devotion. They range from the primitive musings of a twelve-year-old girl on the latest teenybopper idol to the sophisticated musings of a psychologist on the symbolism of the *Star Trek* universe.

The average fan page includes photographs, news, commentary, and interviews related to the subject matter at hand. Fan pages exist for every type of celebrity and art form. TV shows, movies, comic books, actors, musicians and authors all have fans who devote long fan pages to whomever or whatever they admire.

Pick someone or something and do a search on Google (http://www.google.com). Use the terms "fan page" and, say, "Dawson's Creek".

Put quotation marks around search terms that combine two or more words (like fan page).

If you look at a page and you like it, contact the author by e-mail. Just look around the site for the word "contact".

If you don't like the writing style on a site, see if the site has links to other pages on the same subject. A site about the television show *Angel* will often link to other fan sites about *Angel*.

A sub-genre of fan pages is devoted to "fan fiction". People who write fan fiction take the characters and settings of a television show or a movie and write further stories about them. For example, a fan of the show *Friends* might write a story about Joey and Phoebe on a double date where they realize they are in love with each other.

Fan fiction authors obviously love to write and have the time and motivation to do so. You can find an extensive list of links to fan fiction at: http://www.fanfictionlinks.com.

Local Links

When it comes to finding someone local, it's hard, but not impossible.

Not that there aren't plenty of people in your town who have web pages. There are. Some may have even written tens of thousands of beautiful words that would leave you longing to hire them. The trouble is, unless you live in a one-horse town, when you search under just the name of your city, you will receive too many results from businesses.

There are tricks you can use to find someone local on the web, but it takes a bit of work. You have to go through a lot of web pages in order to find someone good.

Here are some ideas to try:

Search under as many cities or towns as are within driving distance. If you live in a small, remote town, meet someone midway. If you are willing to drive two hours and you can find a writer who will drive an hour to meet with you, you can search any area within a three-hour radius of your town.

Click on the link that says "Advanced Search" at Google. Then fill in the space that says, "Find at least one of the following terms." Make sure you use quotes around towns that have names with more than one word, like "Santa Cruz".

In the top box, place the words "personal page" in quotation marks. Click search.

If that doesn't give you enough results, go to Google's main page. Fill in your search box as follows, including the parentheses, replacing the towns I picked with those near you:

("Santa Cruz" OR Aptos OR Capitola OR Watsonville OR "Scotts Valley") AND ("home page" OR "personal home page" OR diary OR journal OR weblog OR blog)

Another possible approach is to try and find someone in your area who has written a fan page. You can search under nearby towns and "fan page".

Sports fans create web pages, too, *about local teams.* The author of a well-written team page is a good candidate to collaborate with you.

http://www.geocities.com/dibears101.geo/index lists links to fan pages for all the major league baseball, football, basketball and hockey teams.

Though this is a great site with hundreds of links, it is not complete. You won't find, for example, the marvelously written Orioles Warehouse page here. As I mentioned before, check the links page on each site you visit. You might find a sites that aren't mentioned on the list.

Is there a college or a university where you live? Many institutions of higher learning have an index that links to the personal pages of students, professors, employees and alumni. Perhaps you will be inspired to collaborate with one of them. An index of 230 such gateways is at http://www.utexas.edu/world/personal.

Not all the links work, and for some universities you won't get in without a password, but this could lead you to a ghostwriter.

Search for links to prominent companies in your area. It's important that the company's *main office* is located in your town. (If you live in Redmond, Washington, don't pick Microsoft. There are too many Microsoft employees who work in other locations.)

Find the URL for the company or the educational institution you plan to check out. Then go to Google's Advanced Search (http://www.google.com/advanced_search?hl=en).

First, change the number of search results by clicking on the arrow next to where it says "10 results". Drag your arrow down and highlight "50 results" then click. This will give you 50 results per page instead of 10.

Scroll down to "Page Specific Search". Fill in the box on the right (next to "Links") with the URL of the company you are searching for. Then click "Search". All the web pages with links to that site will appear. Hopefully that will include talented writers in your area.

College Newspaper Editors And Reporters

Another group of folks worth looking at are reporters and editors for college newspapers. Your best bet is to get them to either a) work your book into their summer vacation plans or b) try to get credit for writing your book as an independent study.

Seniors in their last semester before graduation are also a good option. These folks are good at writing and can meet deadlines. They are, as we are fond of saying in the recruiting business, "young, bright and cheap".

Their main drawback is that they may be unreliable during midterms and finals. The ideal time to approach them is at the end of a semester, before finals start. Complete your negotiations in time to begin your project between semesters.

When school starts again, you will be ready to submit your proposal to agents and publishers. By the time you land a book contract, they can prepare to take a semester off. After all, getting published is a big deal for anyone, especially a college student.

There is a comprehensive web site that lists most college newspapers and links to those that are online. You can find it at: http://newsdirectory.com/college/press/

If your local college paper isn't on the net, just call them.

If it is on the net, browse their page carefully to locate contact information for editors and reporters. If you can't find the folks you want, call the advertising department. Every college newspaper site lists that. Then ask who the editor of the paper is.

As with magazines, always try to recruit the editor first. The editor is more senior than the rest of the people who work for the paper, and has more experience with deadlines and story angles. Plus, if the editor turns you down, you can ask him for referrals to reporters who are both talented and reliable.

Finding Writers In Groups

Writing groups or classes can be found in most counties in America. Some are teacher led; others are groups of peers who critique each other in the hope of becoming better writers.

Groups exist for a variety of genres and sub-genres: fiction, non-fiction, romance, mystery, and poetry. Others are for anyone who writes.

(Yes, I said poetry. Poets are good with words and they can't possibly make a living from poetry. A number of poets have turned to ghostwriting to support their real love. Lyricists are also a possibility, so check out songwriting groups, too.)

You will find people in these groups are often quite talented. They also have a strong commitment to writing. They can bring the work they do with you to their group for feedback. Most people in these groups are unpublished, so you can hire one of them inexpensively.

Here are some places to check for writing groups or classes:

Bulletins for Adult Education
Colleges
The Library (call the reference desk)

Bookstores
The calendar section of your newspaper or your local weekly
Flyers on coffee house bulletin boards (and ask the person behind the counter, too).

If you find a group that's privately led, call the leader and ask her to refer you to a few people who might be appropriate for your project. Then ask who she would call first, second, etc.

With a college or adult education class, attend the class and ask the teacher afterwards for recommendations.

If you find a peer led group, attend the group and see whose writing and personality you like (you will have to work with this person), then approach her.

Most of these writers work at other jobs. Since they already have their own projects, you may not strike pay dirt with the first one you talk to.

ONE OTHER NOTE: One writer may stand out as the best in the group. If you don't succeed in wooing him to work with you, move on to someone else whose work you like. Most non-fiction books live or die based on their content, not how well they are written. You only need a good writer, not a superstar.

A FINAL APPROACH

If you can't locate a writer using the above methods, just try to find someone who likes to write. That could be the woman who puts together your church bulletin or an English teacher at your daughter's high school. (If you work with an English teacher, make sure he is willing and able to write in a conversational style.)

Make sure he can put together a three page sample of his writing so you can judge his work.

If you like it, let him write an outline and a sample chapter with you.

The 0 for 5 Rule: If hiring a writer seems hard, your current idea isn't commercial enough. . If you meet with five writers and none of them want to work on a book based on the idea you have, give up. Find something else to work on.

If you are determined to write on a particular topic come hell or high water, write it yourself with the help of a professional writing coach. See Chapter 11.

CHAPTER 10

THE HIRING PROCESS

The first step in the hiring process is to review writing samples from your potential collaborator. Two samples should be enough. If necessary, one will do.

When you look at them, make sure they keep your interest and flow well. They should sound as smooth as a magazine article or a book. *The tone should be conversational, not formal and stilted.*

WHAT NOT TO WORRY ABOUT: Much of what your English teacher taught you is wrong when it comes to writing for the general population. Don't worry about dangling prepositions or incomplete sentences. That's the way people talk and it sounds like normal speech.

REASONS FOR CONCERN: Spelling errors should be a cause of alarm. Other mistakes that should raise hackles for you are punctuation errors, subject and verbs that don't agree, and improper use of adjectives and adverbs. (If you don't know these things yourself, go with your ear, read a grammar book or hire a writing coach to screen writing samples for you.)

Once you decide you like a writer's work, interview him.

During the interview, you have two jobs—to find out if the writer is someone you want to collaborate with and selling him on you and your book idea. (You want to work with a writer who believes in your book, right?)

Here is what you need to know about the writer you are interviewing:

1) **Can he do it?** Does he have the time and the ability? If he is a professional ghostwriter, how many books is he currently working on? How many does he usually work on? Can he make you a priority? Does he have the drive necessary to take you to the finish line? Does he meet deadlines? If he hasn't written books in the past, what has he done that shows these traits?

2) **Is he easy to collaborate with?** Is he flexible? Can he compromise? Is he willing to let you be the senior decision maker? What have his previous collaborations been like, in terms of writing or other projects? What has he liked and disliked about them?

3) **What's the chemistry like?** What does it feel like to talk with him? Are you comfortable? Is the conversation balanced? Does he seem comfortable with you? Is he interested in your subject matter? Does he "get" your concept? Is he enthusiastic about this project and about you?

An interview is a microcosm of what a person is like to work with.

If he is late for the interview, unless there were unusual circumstances, he will be late for all of your meetings. If he is judgmental about past working relationships, he will be judgmental about you.

On the other hand, if he is prompt, easy going and tolerant, he will probably continue to behave that way throughout your working relationship.

If you are working with an Established Ghostwriter: Interview at least three writers. Ask them if they have relationships with editors and publishers who are potential buyers for your book. If they have published books under their own name, ask if they have any contacts in radio and television. See if they have any freelance experience with magazines that would fit the subject of your book.

SELLING A POTENTIAL COLLABORATOR ON YOUR BOOK

Your collaborator wants to know the same thing any agent or book publisher wants to know: Is this a book that can sell?

Tell him some of the same things you will say in your book proposal.

Answer the following questions to create your sales pitch. (Read Section II of this book for detailed help):

1) **Who are you and why are you qualified to write on this subject?** What kind of experience do you have in this field? Will interviewers for newspapers, radio and television believe that you are a credible expert?

2) **Is there an audience for this book?** Who are they? Why will they be interested? Are there secondary audiences? You can be general on this point, or you can come up with actual statistics. Statistics, of course, are more convincing. (Tools to come up with these statistics are described in Section II.)

3) **What's the competition like and how will your book be different?** Do a quick search on Amazon.com using a word or two that is the general subject of your book. What are the other books that cover this subject? Which one is selling the most? What will your book do better or differently from the rest?

4) **What will you do to make sure this book sells?** Do you have a ready-made audience for your book from your own website, ezine, newsletter, seminars, newspaper or magazine column, or radio or television show? What will you do to publicize this book? Do you plan on spending any of your own money on book promotion?

Bring up your experience and the audience for your subject at the beginning of the interview. You can save the competition and marketing information for when you know this potential collaborator is in the running for the job. The answers you come up with at this stage will help you later with your book proposal. And if you are strapped for cash, the more persuasive your sales pitch, the better your chance of convincing a more experienced writer to take less money upfront.

NEGOTIATIONS

Once you and a collaborator have decided you'll feel comfortable working together, it's time to sort out the details about money issues, credit, etc. Here is a checklist of the issues you need to agree on and put in writing:

1) **Duties** – How will the duties of this book be divided? Who makes the final decisions? Who selects which agents and publishers are to receive the book proposal? Who writes and sends out query letters? Who meets with editors and agents? What obligation does the writer have if the book is accepted for publication? How will requested revisions be handled?

2) **Availability & Schedule** – How much time should each party expect the other to be available? How long will the book proposal take? What is the minimum number of pages to be written each month?

3) **The test phase** – Will there be a test phase? What will you pay during this time? What happens if you decide you are unhappy with the results? Will the fee be paid all at once or will it be based on reaching certain milestones? What will those milestones be?

4) **The fee** – What will the fee be for the book proposal? Will it be hourly or a flat fee? If there is an hourly fee, is there a cap, or at least an estimated worst-case scenario? What will the fee be for writing the rest of the book? If you are basing this payment on a percentage of a hoped for book advance, what happens if the book advance is smaller than you expect? What if you decide to market the book to small publishers or self-publish and there is no advance?

5) **Royalties & Other Income** – Will your collaborator share in royalties? If so, what percentage will she receive? Will the percentage remain constant, or change based on sales or time? If your collaborator does not share in royalties, will there be bonuses based on sales? Will other income be shared in the same manner as royalties?

6) **Credit & Copyright** – How will your collaborator be credited for her work? On the cover, on the title page, in the acknowledgements, or not at all? If she is to get credit on the cover or title page, what words will be used? How big will her name be? If you will thank her in the acknowledgements, what is the minimum you will say? If you change this, does she have approval rights? Also, who owns the copyright to this work?

7) **Breaking Up** – What happens if you break up before you complete the book? What if an agent or publisher suggests that you collaborate with someone else? Who owns what? Who gets paid what?

Write down the answers to each of these questions. They will form the basis for your written agreement.

Let's discuss each of these items in detail.

DUTIES

Though the answers to some of the questions under this heading seem obvious, it is important that they be discussed ahead of time. Write your conclusions down. Otherwise, you both could be working under different assumptions.

The division of labor should be simple. You are responsible for the content of the book proposal, and ultimately the book. It is your collaborator's duty to get it on paper.

On occasion, there might be some room for the writer to get a little creative. When I collaborated on the hair color book, we had a chapter on Avant-Garde hair, which was our fancy name for the punk hairstyles that were popular back then. (We hoped this name would have a longer life than "punk" when it came to hair.)

After the Nardi brothers described a few of their hair coloring recipes, I made up several of my own with names like "Somewhere Over the Rainbow" and "The Zebra". This was fine with them, though they were the true authors of the book.

If they didn't like my contribution, however, they had every right to demand that it be excised.

Since you are the primary author of the book, you get to make all the final decisions. Again, make sure you communicate this in the beginning, and write it down.

If your financial arrangements allow you to, let your writer pick which agents and publishers to submit your sample work to. By the time you reach that stage, she will be an expert in that process, if she isn't already. You can give her some guidelines and overrule her if you disagree. But you don't need to spend a lot of time on this.

Authors send query letters to agents and publishers to get them interested in their book before they send in their proposal. Who should write and send out your query letters? Your writer, since writing quality is one of the main things queries are judged on.

Make sure you specify how long the writer is required to send these out. Some writers will send queries out as long as there is an agent or publisher left who is appropriate for the type of work being submitted. Of course, they may also continue to charge a significant and ongoing monthly fee. Put your expectations with regard to query letters in writing so there are no misunderstandings later.

When your book is accepted for publication, you'll both be ready to celebrate, right?

Not necessarily. What if your collaborator has developed new projects that pay more? What if your advance isn't what you were hoping for, or worse than that (for your writer), you are published by a smaller publisher who, instead of giving you an advance, puts the money into promoting your book

Make sure your partner is obligated to finish the book he has agreed to write with you. Make note of this in your contract. (You can always release him from this obligation if you are in a generous mood or he can be replaced without diminishing your book.)

As you write your book together, you will have meetings scheduled with your editor. Make sure you are both always present. Again, your writer may have other opportunities that draw his attention before your book is complete. Even so, he must attend all of these meetings. You also want to make sure you are included in all meetings with your editor about your book. This way you both hear all instructions, etc., first-hand. Though both of these items seem obvious, include them in your collaboration agreement.

Finally, when you hand in what you think is your final draft, your editor is likely to come back to you with a request for revisions. Make sure that a) you are informed of and approve all   revisions and b) your writer revises as necessary in a timely fashion.

AVAILABILITY & SCHEDULE

Your collaborator needs to be available to you for a certain number of hours each month. And, to be fair, you need to be available to her, too, especially if she has agreed to work for lousy pay or on spec. Your agreement should include a certain minimum time obligation for both of you. This way, if either one of you is not as available as projected, the other one will be free to work with other people or projects.

Have an anticipated schedule. The outline and sample chapters should take about forty-five days. Also, if you are paying the writer on an hourly basis, agree on an estimated maximum number of hours. Most people use one hundred as a likely figure. If it is going to take longer in either days or hours, it is only fair that you be warned.

When you sign a publishing contract, there is a clause that gives a due date for the book. If you decide to self-publish, your agreement with your writer should include a similar statement. If you work with a writer on a retained basis, include an estimate as to how many pages she is expected to write each month.

THE TEST PHASE

Sometimes the most qualified, highly recommended people are unable to offer their best work at a particular time.

Back in 1989, when my wife, Uma, was pregnant, we wanted a nurse-midwife to deliver our baby. After interviewing three with the best reputations, we picked Belinda, (not her real name).

After about two months, Uma, due to morning sickness, could no longer keep even water down. We called Belinda. Though my wife mentioned she was becoming dehydrated, Belinda acted completely unconcerned.

When I finally took my wife to the doctor, she was put on intravenous fluids.

That episode convinced us to switch to another practitioner.

We heard later that Belinda was burnt out from all her years as a nurse-midwife at the beginning of Uma's pregnancy and desperately needed a sabbatical. Within a few months of our experience with her, she took one.

Fortunately, we were free to leave Belinda whenever we chose. If a contract were involved, though, it would have been a different matter.

Keep this story in mind when you select a writer. No matter how great his work has been, there is no guarantee you'll be comfortable working with him or even like what he writes with you.

A test phase, or probationary period, allows you to see how you work together before you commit to a long-term relationship with a writer. Three obvious times to decide if your collaboration is working are:

1) When the outline for your book is finished
2) After the first sample chapter is done
3) When the book proposal is complete

The outline is your first opportunity to decide whether you have made a good hire. It lets you know whether the writer you chose can turn your idea into a full-length book. (Of course, this works both ways. It also lets him know whether you really have enough material to fill a book.)

The first sample chapter allows you to see how your collaborator takes your words and transforms them into print. This initial experience is a likely microcosm of your future together. Do you like what you see? Does it flow? Is it easy to understand? Did your ghostwriter understand what was important and what was less so? Did he use words or expressions that you use, so that the chapter has your voice in it?

If so, keep going.

If not, tell the writer what needs fixing and let him do a rewrite. If he gives you a hard time about it, or if his next draft still has problems, end the collaboration and hire someone else.

The finished book proposal is the last test. Are you satisfied with it? Has your working relationship been comfortable? Are you willing to continue it for the next six to eighteen months?

Hopefully, the answer will be yes.

In case you have to end things:

- Make sure the test phase is in the contract. This way your writer knows he gets to write the book only if you are satisfied with the book proposal and the process of writing it.
- Tie payments to milestones. Make it clear that if you end the collaboration after a particular milestone, payment for all the work up to and including that milestone is all the writer will receive.
- If you collaborate with someone who's writing for free until the book is sold, set up a 'kill fee' and pay him a little something, say $50, if he writes at least 15 pages with you. (Kill fee is a magazine term which means a payment to a writer for an article that was requested but won't be published.)

Your implementation of these ideas will differ depending on how you are paying your writer.

Robert Woodcox, the ghostwriter mentioned at the beginning of this book, charges a new client sixty percent of his monthly fee at their first meeting. He interviews them extensively to come up with an outline and thirty pages. When that is written, they meet again. If the client is satisfied, they pay his monthly rate. If they decide not to continue, he refunds half their money.

If you are paying a flat fee, here's how to split up your payments: 25% for the successful completion of an outline, 25% for one sample chapter, and the final 50% upon completion of the proposal.

If you are paying by the hour, place time limits on each of these activities: twenty hours each for the outline and the sample chapter, one hundred hours total for the whole project, unless there is some unforeseen difficulty.

How you handle a kill fee depends on what you say during your negotiations. Put one in your contract, though. If it's necessary to dismiss your writer after the book proposal is finished, a previously drawn outline of what will happen in such circumstances will make it easier for you to take appropriate action.

Here are two suggestions:

If a writer agrees to work for less than her normal fee in exchange for future royalties, offer a kill fee that is 25% of your advance, or $2000, whichever is lower. This would, of course, be contingent upon selling the book. Include a clause that lets you subtract any cost incurred if you need to hire an additional writer to polish the proposal.

If you are paying a writer $500 or less, a $500 kill fee will do.

THE FEE

A variety of prices for writers in each category has already been explored at great length. There are, however, a number of other issues to discuss.

A flat fee is always your best option for the proposal stage. It can take about a hundred hours to write one—but it may only take half as long as that.

If your collaborator is stuck on the idea of an hourly rate, propose a compromise that may work out in her favor. Base the flat fee on eighty-five hours. The faster the writer, the better this will work out for her. And even if you end up paying a little extra, at least you won't suffer a tremendous cost overrun.

If you have no choice but to pay an hourly fee, ask the writer to agree to stop and show you what she has completed after every twenty hours of work. Make sure there is a clause in your agreement that lets you end the collaboration at any of these junctures.

Once you agree on a price for the proposal, discuss the fee for the rest of your book.

Hopefully, you will land a book contract with a fat enough advance to satisfy your needs and those of your collaborator.

But what happens if you are successful in getting a publishing deal and the advance is thinner than you were expecting?

A friend of mine ran into this very situation. Al was approached by another writer, Joe, to collaborate on a sports book with him. They worked together to develop a book proposal and sent it off to Joe's agent. He submitted it to fifteen publishers, and didn't get a favorable response, so they dropped the project. Al and Joe went their separate ways.

A year later, Joe heard about a publisher who was looking for books like the one he and Al had written. He submitted their proposal and was offered a book contract.

The advance was less than Joe had hoped for. He called Al to let know him know that he wanted to write the book alone.

Al was fine with this, but since they had both worked on spec, he believed that Joe owed him compensation for writing a book proposal that sold.

Joe wasn't getting much of an advance, but Al argued that $5000 was the going rate for a book proposal (at that time) and that he was entitled to that much since he was not going to reap any of the benefits of writing the book.

Joe was pretty upset about this, particularly since he was already writing this book for very little money. Fortunately for Al, Joe's agent agreed that Joe owed Al payment, and eventually Al was paid $4000. But the friendship Al and Joe had developed when they wrote together ended.

THE MORAL OF THE STORY: Prepare for the possibility that your advance will be less than you hope for.

If you are working with an Unheralded Superstar or a senior Established Ghostwriter, most publishers will give you a large enough advance to cover your ghostwriter's fee. If there is a shortfall, however, you will be responsible for whatever you agreed to in your contract.

You are more likely to run into this situation with a less experienced writer.

As you put together your agreement, think about these two questions:

- Are you willing to give up your whole advance in order to get published?
- Would you dig into your own pocket to make this happen?

When you know those answers, ask your *collaborator* the following, as applicable:

1) What is the least you expect to be paid for writing the whole book?
2) What if your share of the advance falls below that?
3) Let's pretend I agree to pay you the entire advance to cover your fee. What if the advance falls below that? Would the opportunity to have a published book be worth writing for a little less money?
4) What if we receive an offer from a publisher that doesn't give an advance? Would you be willing to work for just royalties?

Depending on what each of you answers, you may need to:

- Write with another collaborator after your proposal is accepted by a publisher

-OR-

- Look for a ghostwriter you can afford to hire for the whole book.

Make sure you include whatever the two of you agree will occur under each of these special circumstances in your agreement.

ROYALTIES

Royalties are simple matter to negotiate. Many authors offer their collaborators a certain percentage of the royalties, up to 50%, for the life of the book.

Here is a secret, though. Most authors don't earn more than their book advance. It is estimated that 3 in 10 books make money, 4 in 10 break even, and 3 in 10 lose money.

That means 70% of the time authors don't earn any royalties. But, as we mentioned in Chapter 3, a book is still extremely lucrative because of the many opportunities it brings to you.

So you can afford to be generous when you negotiate royalties with your ghostwriter. They won't make a huge difference in your profits unless you are extremely successful.

And if you are that successful with your book, your subsidiary income from speeches, workshops, etc., will outstrip any money your generosity will have cost you.

How do you decide what percentage of the royalties to offer your ghostwriter?

1) **The more experienced your ghostwriter, the more likely she'll have a set policy regarding royalties.** With top Established Ghostwriters, it's not even an option to offer less than half the royalties. She will tell you what she expects.

2) **The greater the risk your ghostwriter takes, the greater her share of the royalties should be.** If you convince a freelance writer or an editor to write with you for less than her usual fee, reward her with half of the royalties. If a Future Expert is gambling a hundred hours of work on spec to write a proposal with you, give him 25% of the royalties.

3) **The more research and time you expect your ghostwriter to spend on your book, the greater percentage of royalties you should pay her.** Some people have an idea for a book and leave all the research and interviews to their ghostwriter. The author's input is only the basic concept. Their ghostwriters should be generously compensated.

4) **If you are paying a Future Expert a fair wage for writing your book or proposal, he should only receive a small amount of the royalties.** A fair wage for a Future Expert on a book proposal is $500. For a whole book, $3500 to $4000 is right. Since you are giving him a tremendous career opportunity and paying him a reasonable amount, despite his lack of experience, 10% of the royalties is a fair amount.

5) **Plan for a home run.** If you are paying your ghostwriter a flat fee, make some provisions to share the wealth if your book becomes a runaway bestseller. If it sells more than a hundred thousand copies, give your writer a $10,000 cash bonus and 10% of the royalties from that point on. Share the wealth. After all, a successful book will put you in the 50% tax bracket; so half of what you'll pay your collaborator at that point would go to taxes, anyway. If your book is *that* successful, it will be due, in some part, to your ghostwriter.

This last point relates to what occurred with Lee Iacocca's autobiography, *Iacocca*.

William Novak, Iacocca's collaborator, wasn't really underpaid. He earned $40,000 for writing a business autobiography. If it sold as expected, that would have been reasonable pay.

But no one anticipated America's interest in the man who saved Chrysler from bankruptcy. Maybe it was because Honda and Toyota were noticeably robbing customers from American automakers at the time. Maybe it was due to Iacocca's phoenix-like comeback after getting fired by Ford. Whatever the reason, people loved his story. *Iacocca* jumped to number one the first week it was published.

At this writing, there are nearly *seven million* copies of *Iacocca* in print. Lee Iacocca has made at least ten million dollars from sales of the book alone. Add in tapes, speaking fees, the huge advance he received for his next book, *Talking Straight*, (written with another collaborator, Sonny Kleinfield), and it is obvious that Mr. Iacocca earned millions more.

Next to fifteen or twenty million dollars, forty grand seems like a paltry sum, and Novak complained. He eventually haggled his way to another $40,000 from Iacocca. (Don't waste any tears on poor William Novak. He went on to write bestsellers with Tip O'Neill, Nancy Reagan, Oliver North and Magic Johnson.)

If you are successful beyond your wildest dreams, enjoy the ride. And save yourself some aggravation at a time that should be pure revelry. Include your collaborator in your success. Plan for its possibility and write a bonus into your agreement for your collaborator.

OTHER INCOME

Your book may earn income for you other than royalties. This income may be derived from items like foreign sales, publishing sections of your book in magazines, and sales to other media like film and television.

The way to handle this in your agreement is to write a statement such as "Joe Smith, the ghostwriter, will receive fifty percent (50 %) of all royalties and all other income from this book." Or, "Joe Smith, the ghostwriter, will receive only a flat fee. He will not receive a share of any other income derived from this book." (Author's disclaimer: I am not a lawyer and cannot give out legal advice. Have your lawyer review any contract you put together.)

CREDIT

How do you decide how to credit your collaborator for her work?

Think about the needs of your audience. Will they be disappointed to find out you didn't write your book by yourself? Will they be less likely to buy it? Will sharing credit give you less credibility with your audience and the media?

For most first-time authors, the answer to these questions is no.

There are certain situations, though, where it would be wise to proceed with caution. If you are a therapist writing about a topic with some depth, you are better off listing your writer in the acknowledgements section. That is where you can praise her for helping you take difficult psychological concepts and making them accessible to the general public—thus explaining your use of a second writer in a way that is palatable to your readers (even if the real reason is that you are far too busy with your practice and research to have the time to write a book by yourself.).

Professors are another group that should keep their non-academic collaborators off the cover. The world likes to think of professors as extra smart with lots of time to sit and think. If you are a professor, give generous credit to your ghostwriter—but save it for the acknowledgements section of your book.

Medical doctors, on the other hand, can share their glory with no damage at all. Doctors have their practices and research to contend with. Everybody knows that doctors are too busy to write— (and even if they had the time, who could read their handwriting? Ba-dum dum.)

Also, consider your own need for credit, without concern for anyone or anything else. Do you want all the credit for your book, or would you feel more comfortable sharing it? How will you feel if the world knows, from the cover of your book, that it was "ghostwritten"? Though the terminology would technically be incorrect—(due to your generosity, your collaborator would be a co-author, not a ghost)—this is what some people, particularly the jealous ones, just at the edge of your personal radar screen, will say.

Finally, if one of your goals is to attract business with your book, consider whether sharing credit will affect your status with potential customers.

If you decide to put your collaborator's name on the cover, the various ways to do that are discussed in Chapter 2.

Another approach is to list your ghostwriter on the title page of your book. This is especially useful if there is more than one author to list, as was the case with my first book, *Color Your Hair Like A Pro*. Adding "with Steven M. Grossman" (my birth name--I have since changed it) to "By Vincent and Fred Nardi" would have ruined the design for the book cover, which had the Nardis' names at its very bottom, in large print strewn across its entire length.

But adding "with Steven M. Grossman" to the title page was completely fine with me. I still had something I could show friends, relatives and future employers, which is all I cared about. And the Nardis had a book that looked, for most purposes, like they wrote it themselves. Who really looks that closely at the title page unless it's pointed it out to them?

But if you want to be surreptitious about the fact that you are using a ghostwriter, just offer a thank you in the acknowledgements of the book. Your collaborator, especially if she's a first-time ghostwriter, will feel more comfortable if you add something to your contract that states the minimum wording you will use. Add a statement like "Harriet Keller will be thanked in the acknowledgements of this book 'for her help with organizing the book'. Any other description of her services will require her approval in writing."

COPYRIGHT

It is essential that you include this sentence in your contract: "The copyright for this work belongs to the Author."

BREAKING UP

This is a subject that MUST be addressed in your contract. You can run into all kinds of trouble if you don't.

About twenty years ago, I was in a songwriting workshop with a lyricist who was put in a difficult situation because of good news from a music publisher.

The publisher told her she had written terrific lyrics that could easily be a hit—but that the music by her composer wasn't strong enough. What made this especially frustrating for her was that this would be her first 'published' song if it had the right music. (A publisher in the music industry is like an agent in the book business.) The publisher had several composers on staff with a track record of composing hits.

Most amateur songwriters write together on a handshake. There's never a contract. And they certainly never discuss the possibility that one partner will want new music for her lyrics, or vice versa. My acquaintance was no exception. She didn't know what to do.

If she had an agreement that included clauses about breaking up, she might have been able to make the move that was in her best interest—finding another composer.

I never learned how things turned out for her, but I hoped she was successful. The song she wrote was called "Why do Bad Boys Make Me Feel So Good?"

Five or six years later, I heard a song on the radio that made me both excited and jealous.

The chorus was: "Bad, bad, bad, bad boys make me feel so good".

The song "Bad Boys" was a huge hit for Gloria Estefan and the Miami Sound Machine.

Happy ending, right?

Wrong. I called up BMI, the agency that collects royalties for songwriters from radio airplay, and found out that song was written by Larry Dermer, Joe Galdo, and Rafael Vigel.

No women's names on that list. It wasn't her song! (By the way, don't think these other songwriters stole her idea. "Bad boys make me feel so good" is exactly the kind of title a good songwriter comes up with. Good girls falling for bad boys is hardly a new concept and using opposites in a title is a common songwriting technique.)

My acquaintance got half of the puzzle right. With a song like that, the title is everything.

If she had looked for someone else to write new music for her lyric, *her song* could have been the one that was *on the radio*.

And as hard as it would have been for my friend to fire her composer, it would have been easier if she had an agreement that included a breakup clause.

Can the same kind of thing happen to you in the literary world?
Absolutely.

Imagine submitting your book proposal to an agent or an editor who loves your idea. She views you as a credible expert on your topic. There is one catch—she says the writing isn't up to professional standards and that you need a different ghostwriter.

This really does happen.

Hopefully, if you follow the instructions in this book, it won't happen to you. But protect yourself just in case it does.

Be certain your agreement covers who owns what if you break up. Make sure it says that you have all the rights to the ideas.

Remember, it is your book, based on your experience.

Dan Poynter, the self-publishing guru and author of *Is There A Book Inside You?* suggests this wording. (He, too, advises that he isn't a lawyer, and that any agreement be vetted by one):

> "Writer agrees not to use information gained during the preparation of this work to write any competitive work on the same or any allied subject. Writer acknowledges that all confidential ideas for the book are supplied by the Author and are the exclusive property of the Author."

These valuable sentences are called a non-compete clause. Use one, even if you are writing memoirs. This way, your ghostwriter can't use your knowledge or experience to write a book that will compete with yours.

You don't want to wind up like Pamela Harriman.

Famous as the U.S. Ambassador to France and for the parties she threw as darling of the Democrats in Washington D.C., Harriman hired Christopher Ogden to write her memoirs. After he spent forty hours interviewing her, she got cold feet. She abandoned the project—without paying Ogden.

This wasn't just unethical—it was stupid. Ogden had forty hours of candid interviews with Harriman on tape—enough material for three books. Ogden swiftly shifted from celebrity's ghostwriter to independent biographer. His book, *The Life of the Party*, with nearly every chapter named for a husband, lover or power broker Harriman knew, spent fourteen weeks on the *New York Times* Bestseller List.

And Ogden's version was a bit more candid than the one the French Ambassador had in mind.

You can avoid these problems.

First of all, do the right thing and pay your writer for any work she has done, even if you decide to abort the project. And before you hand her a check, get your interview tapes back!

But most important of all, include a non-compete clause in your contract.

SPECIAL NOTES FOR SELF-PUBLISHERS

If you plan to self-publish your work, there are several additional elements to address in your contract.

Duties: When you self-publish, you do the jobs a regular publisher would normally do. Three of these fall to your writer:

- Creating an index for your book (which is a necessity if you want to sell to libraries).
- Getting permission to use quotes and illustrations from published material. (Jean Marie Stine, author of *Writing Successful Self-Help & How-To Books* and a former editor at Jeremy Tarcher, says you only

need permission if you quote more than two short paragraphs. However, a literary agent I know recommends that his clients get permission for almost every quote—anything more than a short paragraph. And for a song lyric, he suggests getting permission for the use of even one line.)

- Proofreading--*Sans* editor, your ghostwriter is usually your proofreader.

The Test Phase: Since you're the publisher, there's no need for a book proposal. If you don't feel comfortable hiring a writer after just an outline and a test chapter, add one more milestone. This could be two more chapters for the writer to complete, for a total of three, before he is officially hired. Pay him 10% of the agreed upon fee for completing the sample chapter and outline, and an additional 30% when you are satisfied with the third chapter.

Why pay 40% at this juncture, when less than that much has been written?

Up to this point, the writer has shouldered all the risks. When he has passed all your tests and you are certain you want to hire him for the duration of your book, it's your turn to take a small chance.

The Fee: When you self-publish, the fee is for the whole book, not just a book proposal. How you approach hiring a writer will be modified in a number of ways:

1) Hiring a top of the line writer will come directly out of *your* pocket. With a self-published book, a writer of this status loses most of her value since a) you're already getting published, so her reputation won't help you get in the door, increase your advance, or encourage the publishing house to spend more to promote your book b) she didn't get credit for the bestselling books she has written, so her name won't be any help in publicizing or selling your book. She can, however, write a top-notch book for you.

2) At the opposite end of the spectrum, you are less likely to find someone who will write a whole book just for the experience. A book proposal is short and the hundred or so hours it takes to put one together is a reasonable risk, but a whole book for free is a much greater risk. I hire young writers to create books of about one hundred pages for as little as $2000, and $3000 for books that are twice that size. More experienced freelance writers charge more than double those fees.

   But no matter who I hire, I do a lot of work as an editor to guarantee that the book has the appropriate content and style. So you may be better off paying more money for a writer with actual experience creating a whole book.

3) Royalties are a hassle in this situation. It's better for you and your writer to avoid them. You don't want the difficulty of keeping track of them and she won't want to worry about whether she's getting all she's entitled to. Without royalties, though, you may have to pay her more.

   If you are printing a thousand books or less, there is an alternative to royalties: pay your writer a certain amount per copy when you reprint the book. If you order a second print run of an additional two thousand books and you give fifty cents a book to your writer, you'll pay out an additional $1000. But this may be more affordable after you've sold

your first thousand books (say at $15 apiece) than before you print your
first run of books.

4) Your safest solution is to hire a writer with two books behind him. This
will cost you $25,000 to $35,000.

5) The best tradeoff of cost versus experience, even for a self-published
book, remains magazine editors. The likely cost for an entire book is
$7000 to $15,000. If budget is a major issue for you, don't worry about
finding an editor who is nearby. Contact several throughout the
continent until you find someone in your price range. Make sure this
person writes in a style you enjoy and is someone you get along with.

6) If you are working with a less experienced writer, set some money aside
to implement the ideas in Chapter 11, Insurance Policies.

Royalties & Other Income: If for some reason you must award royalties to
your collaborator, the split is different when you are the publisher.

An author gets paid a small percentage of the price on the cover of the book.
Since you are the publisher, you won't be splitting the profits fifty-fifty with your
collaborator. Instead, you will pay her half or less of the royalties a traditional
publisher will pay to an author:

For *hardcover books*, royalties are typically 10% of the first 5000 sold, 12.5%
for the next 5000, and 15% after that. Since almost all sales of your book will result
solely from your promotional efforts, don't pay your collaborator more than 5% for
hardcover royalties.

Trade paperbacks are the large sized books you find in bookstores for $15 to
$22. Royalties for these average 7.5%. 3% should be enough to keep your
ghostwriter happy.

Mass market paperbacks are the cheaper, smaller books lined up on your
supermarket's front wall. Royalties start at 6% for these. Pay your ghostwriter no
more than 3% per book sold.

All other income from your book should accrue only to you, as the author and
publisher.

CHAPTER 11

INSURANCE POLICIES

Unless you are working with an Established Ghostwriter or an Unheralded Superstar, save part of your budget to run your book or proposal by the most experienced publishing professional you can afford. Here are four options, ranging from $200 an hour to absolutely free. The more you pay, the more qualified (and possibly connected) a consultant you can hire. But no matter what you can afford, use one of the following options to appraise the quality of the work you and your collaborator have done.

EDITORIAL SERVICES

Editorial services provide full critiques for writers, starting with the book concept, and then working through each segment of your proposal with a fine-tooth comb, line by line. They charge as much as $200 per hour. They are worth the price they charge; the majority of them are owned and run by individuals who have been editors at large publishing houses. Not only have these publishing professionals been on the receiving side of the desk for thousands of book proposals--they were also colleagues with many editors who are still working today. They have a clear sense of what editors like and what will make them throw a manuscript in the trash.
Some of these freelance editors have friends who are still in the business and will act as your agent if they know your book will appeal to a certain editor.

Don't hesitate to agree to this opportunity, should it come up. These folks used to be the ones behind the desks offering book contracts to first-time authors, so they know exactly what they can extract from a publisher for your book.

The best place to look for editorial services is in the classified section of magazines for writers, like *The Writer* or *Writer's Digest*. If you can't find these monthlies at your local bookstore, you can subscribe to them at http://www.writermag.com and http://www.writersdigest.com.

In both magazines, the classified ads are in the back of the magazine. In *The Writer*, look under "CRITIQUING/EDITING" on the page where the classifieds start.

The section to browse in *Writer's Digest* is "EDITING/REVISING". It starts with text ads, and is usually followed by a full-page ad. Turn the page and you'll see that this section continues with display ads. The editors who spend a little extra for the display ads are usually the ones who are the most qualified.

One of the ads you will see is for Mark Chimsky Editorial Plus. Mark has headed major imprints and edited national bestsellers. He says it can be a good idea to speak with a freelance editor *before* you start a project:

"Working early on with an experienced editor to crystallize the shape
and direction of a work can help a writer to gain perspective on the best
course to take . . . [These] professionals have a clear understanding of
what publishers are looking for in today's marketplace."

WRITING COACHES

Writing coaches are either writers with published books or very senior magazine
editors.

They charge between one and two hundred dollars an hour. Writing coaches can
offer you the perspective of a successfully published writer at a lower cost than a
freelance editor. They may have some industry contacts, but not as many as
freelance editors.

Save money by using a coach to offer you big picture suggestions. Leave the
line editing (going through your book line by line to check for errors) to someone
less expensive.

You can find writing coaches under "Critiquing" in the back of *Writer's Digest*.
You can also approach any Established Ghostwriter for the same kind of help.

I would be neglecting my duties if I didn't mention that my company, **THE
AUTHORS TEAM**, provides coaching and editing for writers. We also perform
"Book Proposal Diagnostics".

We can be reached at (866) 7-AUTHOR. E-mail us at
GetPublished@AuthorsTeam.com. Our home on the web is:
http://www.AuthorsTeam.com

LINE EDITORS

If your book proposal has frequent errors in spelling, grammar, or style, you are
doomed. An editor will cast it aside before he's finished reading the first page. If
your work is polished, though, you stand out as a professional. (Don't have a heart
attack, though, if after you send off your book proposal, you discover two or three
typos that you somehow missed. Editors can tell the difference between a one-time
typo and repeated misspellings.)

An inexpensive way to have a professional line edit your book proposal is to
contact the magazine editors we talked about earlier. Since it is likely that they earn
around $20 per hour, you can probably hire one for about $25 an hour as a
consultant. Or you can suggest a flat fee. The usual rate is about two dollars per
page, so you're getting a good deal at a hundred dollars or less for a 50 page
proposal.

COLLEGE STUDENTS

If you want to keep your costs to $50 or less for line editing, college students are
your best bet.

A college newspaper editor is not just a good choice for a ghostwriter—he
would also do fine as a line editor, too. So would the reporters who work for him. As

mentioned previously, a web site that lists most college newspapers and links to the ones that are online is at: http://newsdirectory.com/college/press/. Go back to Chapter 9 for more detailed information about contacting these folks.

You can also place a listing on college job boards. Ask the applicants to give you a professor as a reference.

THE TEN FRIENDS TECHNIQUE

If you can't afford to hire someone to edit your book, give your book proposal to ten people with good writing or communication skills and ask them to go through it with a fine-toothed comb looking for mistakes in spelling and grammar. While one person might not pick up everything, ten people will.

Ask them to also mention if there are passages, (particularly instructions), that are difficult to understand. If two or more people have trouble with the same section, have it rewritten.

CHAPTER 12

MISCELLANEOUS TIPS

One way to save money, particularly if you are paying a writer an hourly rate, is to have all of your interviews transcribed. This will also get your book or proposal finished more quickly. The least expensive transcription service I know of is at http://www.idictate.com. They charge a penny per word and guarantee they will e-mail your document to you within twenty-four hours. I have sent them material at midnight and gotten it back just four hours later. I don't know how they do it. Maybe they have typists in China.

The average book is about seventy-five thousand words, so it is theoretically possible to dictate an entire tome for just $750. (Author Rick Crandall says that one hour of speaking is comprised of five or six thousand words, about the length of one book chapter. Based on his estimations, this would take you between twelve and fifteen hours of continuous talk.)

You can also hire a college student for transcription. If you pay him $8 per hour, he will have to be able to transcribe at least 800 words per hour to be on par with Idictate.

Here are two ways to make sure your book sounds like you: When Mark Steisel conducts interviews with the authors he works with, he always wears a headset and types phrases that he will want use later to help his writing achieve the author's voice. Be certain your ghostwriter does this, too.

You can make your book sound uniquely yours by using parenthetical comments. (I hate using technical writing jargon-- but sometimes you just have to!) A parenthetical comment is an observation you make directly to your readers, surrounded by parentheses, that comments on what the reader just read. It works best if it's personal, or if it refers to a story or character previously mentioned. Self-deprecation can raise the parenthetical comment to an art form. Of course, you can take it too far, if you do it with the wrong audience.

Why does the parenthetical comment work so well? Because it gives you a sense that you are the author's confidant. It's as if the writer is taking you aside, putting his arm around your shoulder, and quietly telling *just you* something personal that acknowledges your special relationship with him. (At least that's how it feels to me. Should I be embarrassed?)

It is imperative that you stay current on your topic. Here are two ways to keep up for (almost) free:

LexisNexis has the most extensive database of newspapers and magazines in the world. You can search here for any new articles in your subject area. Instead of buying the article from LexisNexis, though, just search on Google for the publication in which the article appears. Then find the search box for the publication, input your search term, and hit the button that starts the search. Your article should appear, for free. (To keep your account open with LexisNexis, you need to buy one article, for as little as $3.00, every 120 days. Or you can establish a new account every four months.)

The second way to keep up on your subject is a bit simpler. A service, from Google, called Google News, promises to "search and browse 4,000 continuously updated news sources" at: http://www.news.google.com. Just fill in your search term and click.

Use Google News in addition to LexisNexis. Since Google News performs web-based searches, you'll find articles here before they show up on LexisNexis.

I am a big fan of the TV show *American Idol*. I read on the web that they named Kristin Holt, one of their semi-finalists, as a co-host for their 2003 edition. I wanted to find out what song she had sung in the semi-finals of the show, to help me remember which singer she was. I checked LexisNexis for articles, but there weren't any. Google News, however, had two articles listed.

Use these same two services to create a terrific press list.

When you find articles on your topic, make a list of the periodicals they appear in and the reporters who wrote them. Contact these same journalists when your book comes out to see if they will write about you.

A Cautionary Note: Inexpensive ghostwriters aren't miracle workers.

In order to write a book with a ghostwriter, an author needs to have something to say, even if it's pretty much the same thing everyone else says. Otherwise a ghostwriter will have nothing to work with. (You can hire a ghostwriter to write a book from just her research, but it will be quite expensive.)

After I had worked with two authors who really knew what they were talking about, my agent made the mistake of asking me to do a book proposal (for free) for a friend of hers.

Ted, (not his real name), was a buyer of men's clothing for a major department store and wanted to write a guide to dressing right for men.

If you knew me back then, (and even now), you would know that I graduated from the Homer Simpson School of Haberdashery.

I had nothing to suggest on this topic from personal experience.

Ted and I developed an outline for his book, which was easy— one chapter for each article of clothing that a man wears. I created catchy chapter titles like "Best Foot Forward" for shoes, and "In Sheep's Clothes" for sweaters.

We had seventeen chapters set up. At 11 or 12 pages per chapter, writing a book was going to be no sweat.

Our next job was to work on was the sample chapters. Usually, that includes an introduction as to why the author is writing the book and one or two other chapters.

I tried to get Ted to explain why he wanted to write this book. He didn't have much to say, so we moved on to the sample chapter.

I figured I would grill him about the various pieces of clothing we planned chapters about, starting with the easiest one first— the tie. Of all the elements that make up men's couture, the tie is the one that most men know the most about.

Not Ted, though. He had about two sentences, at the most.

Ties are small, I thought to myself. Maybe if I pick something bigger, he'd have more to say.

"How about sports jackets?" I asked, gingerly.

Two more sentences issued from his mouth. Then, more silence.

"Shoes?"

Nothing.

"Sweaters?"

Nothing

"Socks?"

"Underwear?"

"Suits?"

(Maybe a lawsuit would get him to say enough to fill a chapter.)

Ted had two sentences to spare on each of these subjects.

I didn't know then what I know now, so instead of calling my agent and telling her that when it came to men's fashion, this guy couldn't write a postcard, let alone a book, I did my best, wrote a thin book proposal, and sent it off.

This was a huge mistake. Not only did I never write a book on men's fashion, sending this proposal eventually led to the dissolution of my relationship with the agent, as well as the end of her longstanding friendship with Ted, who believed it was her fault that he didn't ever get published.

The moral of the story is this: If you are hiring a writer on spec for very little pay, you have to contribute something to the collaboration. You can't have him do all the thinking and the writing for you. *If you want to be a published author, you need to have something to say!*

But even if you have something to say and you hire a ghostwriter who has published half a dozen books, it doesn't guarantee you a book contract.

A woman named Rachel was told by an agent that the material in her book proposal was compelling enough that he *might* be interested in representing her, if she worked with a professional writer.

Rachel hired Janet, a friend of mine with six books published under her own name, to rewrite her book proposal. Janet brought the material up to professional standards and Rachel resubmitted it to the agent.

Unfortunately, when he read the material a second time, though it was presented in a much more skillful manner, the agent decided against representing Rachel.

Rachel decided this was entirely Janet's fault and demanded her money back. But Janet had delivered the work as she was asked to; she refused to return a cent.

Not only did Rachel sue Janet--she started to harass her as well.

One day Janet found Rachel sitting in a parked car just watching Janet's house. Janet called the police.

Luckily, the police officer talked to Rachel and convinced her that, since the issue was going to be resolved by the courts, she should stay away from Janet.

Janet was grateful and relieved when Rachel managed to stay away.

Eventually, a judge dismissed Rachel's case. As was appropriate, Janet got to keep the money.

There are three morals to this story:

1) When an agent or a publisher says they may be interested in your manuscript or your proposal after a rewrite, there is no guarantee that they will take you on as a client. Sometimes cleaning up the writing reveals other flaws in the material that were previously obscured.

2) As mentioned above, just because you hire a professional writer to help write your proposal, there's no guarantee you'll get published.

3) Be careful when you agree to work with any collaborator. No matter what the circumstances, a reference check is essential, especially if you are going to work with someone in your home.

Another implied moral is this: **Don't let your fate rest in the hands of just one person!**

There are lots of agents and publishers with differing points of view. Everyone's taste is different. Everyone's idea of what will sell is different. And everyone's ability to relate to a particular idea is different.

If an agent or an editor doesn't relate to your material, you'll get turned down even if you are Shakespeare.

Literary agent Jillian Manus tells this story: "One of my assistants came to me and said, 'Jillian, this is an unbelievable proposal. I know you won't buy it but you've got to see it. It's hysterical.' So I looked at it, and it was called *Knitting with Dog Hair*. I looked at it and said, 'Knitting with dog hair?' And she said, 'You've got to read it.' I read it and it was all about how you follow little Fluffy or Spot or Fido and you pick up all their little hairs and you knit them into booties or afghans or something like that to make them live with you forever. It was very, very interesting, but obviously I couldn't take it on because I really didn't know the audience, even though this woman included how many dogs, dog owners, and knitters there are. She really, really understood this. Sure enough, I passed on it. It has now sold over 500,000 copies. Thank you. Did I kill myself? Yes, but that's another story."

You don't need everyone in the publishing business to get behind your book. You only need one publisher.

Take heart from the tale of Jack Canfield and Mark Victor Hansen, authors of *Chicken Soup for the Soul*:

> "When we completed the first *Chicken Soup for the Soul* book, it was turned down by thirty-three publishers in New York and another ninety at the American Booksellers Association convention in Anaheim, California before Health Communications, Inc., decided to publish it. All the major New York publishers said, 'It is too nicey-nice' and 'Nobody wants to read a book of short little stories.' Since that time more than 8 million copies of the original *Chicken Soup for the Soul* book have been sold." The series, which has grown to thirty-two titles, in thirty-one languages, has sold more than 82 million copies."

CHAPTER 13

FINAL THOUGHTS ON HIRING A GHOSTWRITER

"If they say it takes a village to raise a child, it truly takes a city, a state, or nation to birth a book."

That's what actress Sela Ward says in the acknowledgements to *Homesick*, her book about growing up in the south.

She adds, " . . . without the assistance . . . of my team, this book would have remained just a dream."

When a celebrity like Ms. Ward even whispers the idea that she wants to write a book, an editor will immediately appear, like a fairy godmother with a team of people ready to help.

But for a regular Joe or Jane, getting assistance is a do-it-yourself job.

So do it yourself.

Put your team together.

Find a ghostwriter.

A ghostwriter can make the difference between a personal story that reaches a few people and a bestseller that touches millions of lives.

Just ask Betty Eadie.

A high-school dropout and the mother of eight, Eadie wrote her book with the help of ghostwriter (and publisher) Curtis Taylor. She says, "Without his extraordinary talent . . . this book would not exist in its present form."

She has earned well into seven figures from the six million copies of *Embraced by the Light* currently in print.

Thousands of people have developed a stronger spiritual connection because of her book. Eadie's affect on her core audience is so profound that she has published a volume of prayers and devotions made up of quotes from her books and their corollaries in the Bible.

You don't need to have the kind of success Betty Eadie had for a published book to have an incredible impact on your income and your life.

But I promise you this: It will have an effect on your life.

Now onto Section II, where you will learn everything you need to know to sell your book for a fat advance from a major publisher.

SECTION II
LAND A BOOK DEAL FROM JUST TWENTY PAGES

What an author likes to write most is his signature on the back of a check.

- Brendan Francis

INTRODUCTION TO SECTION II

The trick to hiring a ghostwriter for little or no money is to convince her that a publisher will pay for the right to publish your book, before you even write it. You, of course, will then pay a fair wage to the ghostwriter from the money the publisher gives you.

How to get publishers to do this is revealed in this section.

Interestingly enough, the same ideas you use to convince a publisher to buy your book are useful in convincing a ghostwriter to work with you, too.

And if you plan on self-publishing, read this section anyway. Putting your book idea through the same process the major publishers do will make it more competitive in the marketplace.

CHAPTER 14

IT AIN'T JUST DUMB LUCK

Publishing expert Jerrold Jenkins estimates that there are six million manuscripts currently in circulation.

Last year 150,000 books were published in the United States, ninety-thousand more than just two years before.

Still, only 2.5% of the manuscripts in circulation actually made it into print.

This book will help you land in that 2.5%.

Follow its instructions carefully and you will get *significant attention* from agents and publishers.

As agent and author Peter Rubie says, "if you have a polished and well-written book idea, you're in competition, not with all the others who submit, but with the 5 to 10 percent whose material cries out to be taken seriously by editors and agents."

THE RIGHT STUFF

My father used to tell me that you could build or fix anything with the right tools.

When it comes to getting published, most people don't use the right tool. The right tool to get an agent or an editor interested in publishing a non-fiction book is called a book proposal. It consists of some marketing information, a one-page biography, and one or two sample chapters.

Even if you have written a complete manuscript, you still need to submit a book proposal first—not the manuscript.

Why do publishing pros want a sample instead of the whole book?

1) **They are incredibly busy.** The major publishing houses receive as many as 5000 book proposals a week. Literary agents get inundated as well. They just don't have time to read complete manuscripts.

2) **Publishers want to know why they should invest in you.** Publishing is a business. More than half of a book proposal is a business plan that explains how and why your book will make money.

3) **Agents and editors may only like part of your idea.** An editor may think, 'gee, if she had written 'x' instead of 'y', I might have been interested. But you won't get that kind of feedback with a complete manuscript. Instead, if it's evaluated at all, it will be evaluated on what's there, not on it's potential. A proposal, on the other hand, allows editors and agents to make suggestions that will make your book easier to sell.

4) **If publishing pros do like your idea, they need it in a form that they can present to other people.** It's obvious that agents need to present

your material to editors. But even editors at the big publishing houses can't buy books on their own. They have to submit them for approval to the whole editorial board, which is comprised of other editors who have their own stacks of proposals to read. These other editors want to see your book idea in a format that will help them make a decision in the least amount of time.

A book proposal offers *major advantages for writers, too.* It takes the average writer about 100 hours to write a book proposal, and 725 hours to write a non-fiction book. If you write something that doesn't sell, (and at some point in your life you will), you are much better off having invested only 100 hours.

And if a publisher only likes part of your idea, you won't have wasted countless hours on material that you will be rewriting.

Here's what happened to Cindy Ventrice, author of *Make Their Day*.

Cindy submitted her book proposal to ten different publishers. Two responded positively. Neither, however, wanted Cindy's book the way she imagined it.

Each publisher had diametrically opposing views as to how Cindy should proceed:

> "My original sample chapters were probably 75% text and then I had little workbook types of examples. And one of the publishers was intrigued by the workbook part. They wanted a proposal based on at least 50% workbook and no more than 50% text."

The other publisher requested that Cindy take most of the workbook material out. They "wanted me to take a very strong stand as far as my opinions of employee recognition were concerned. They were very clear as to what the book would need to look like for them to be interested," says Ventrice.

Ms. Ventrice wrote two new book proposals so she could keep her options open. Both publishers offered her book deals. Ventrice chose the second one. Her book is currently available in bookstores. (By the way, we have a copy of the final proposal for Ventrice's *Make Their Day* in the back of this book.)

THE SECRET FORMULA

Imagine how much work it would have been to write two new manuscripts instead of two different book proposals.

Ms. Ventrice only had to rewrite her outline and sample chapters. The rest of her proposal, which was made up of marketing materials, and her biography, didn't need substantial changes

Actually, the only part of a proposal that becomes part of a final book is the two sample chapters. These will fill up as little as twenty pages of your published book.

That's why this book is called *Land a Book Deal From Just Twenty Pages!*

The ingredients for a book proposal are almost always the same, though their content varies widely:

1) Title Page
2) Endorsements (optional)
3) Table of Contents (for the proposal itself)
4) Overview
5) The Audience
6) The Competition
7) About the Author
8) Publication Particulars (length, format, illustrations, etc.)
9) Promotion Strategies
10) Outline
11) Chapter Summaries
12) Sample Chapters
13) Appendix

Here is what each of these sections contains:

1) THE TITLE PAGE

On first look, this is the simplest part of a book proposal. To complete the title page, type the title and subtitle of your book in the center of the page. Then add your contact information below that. Include your snail mail address, your voice, fax and cell phone numbers, and your e-mail address.

Believe it or not, your title page is one of the most important ingredients in the secret formula. Why? Because it contains your book's title. An irresistible title may mean the difference between getting published and being turned down. It can also increase the size of your advance.

Think about your own behavior in a bookstore. Doesn't a great title make you pick up a book?

If you want to make an editor or an agent eager to read the rest of your proposal, make sure you have a mouthwatering title. It'll propel your proposal to the top of the stack.

2) ENDORSEMENTS (OPTIONAL)

Including endorsements with your book proposal is a very powerful way to make your proposal stand out from the pack, particularly if they come from celebrities, bestselling authors, or prominent people in your field.

3) TABLE OF CONTENTS (FOR THE PROPOSAL)

Simply list the sections of your book proposal and the pages they are on. This will make it easier for anyone who reads it.

4) THE OVERVIEW

The overview is a one to three page miniature version of your book proposal.

This section is just like the first audition for *American Idol*. You've got sixty seconds to prove that your book idea is good enough to "go to Hollywood". If an agent likes what she reads here, she'll read the rest of your proposal. If not, she may move on to the next one in her stack.

Imitate the back of a paperback, starting off with two sentences that hook a reader's attention.

Make sure you include the main benefits and features of your book, who its audience will be, and why they'll buy your book instead of another one that is already published. Add one or two paragraphs that explain why you're especially qualified to be the author of this text.

If there are any endorsements that will be coming your way, mention them here.

Finally, estimate how long your manuscript will be and how much time it will take to complete.

5) THE AUDIENCE

This is an expanded version of some of the ideas covered in the overview. Your job is to prove to an agent or editor that there are enough people interested in the subject matter of this book to make it worth publishing.

First, describe the typical reader; for example, parents of children with A.D.D. Next, describe how this book will solve their problems. (It will help their children use natural products to replace Ritalin, allowing them to enjoy life without feeling drugged, keeping them healthier.) Then describe other people who will also be interested in this book. (Teachers, psychologists, medical professionals, day care providers, and grandparents.)

Once you've described these people and their characteristics, add statistics. If you can find the actual number of Ritalin users, that's great. Include whatever statistics you find about the total number of elementary school teachers, child psychologists, day care workers, etc. If there is a book on A.D.D. that has sold well, mention how many copies it has sold.

One technique commonly used to show the size of an audience is to list all the magazines on a topic and the number of subscribers they have.

6) THE COMPETITION

For this section, answer the following questions:

- How many books compete with yours?
- Have any of these books done well? (The answer to this question should be 'yes'. It's easier to sell a book if other books on the same subject have been successful.)
- Which five or six of these books compete with yours?

- How does your book differ from each of those books? What does your book do better than they do? (Do a case by case assessment of your book's strengths and the competition's weakness.)

7) ABOUT THE AUTHOR

Strut your stuff and show why you are qualified to write on your particular topic here. Also mention your general writing experience. Of particular interest is anything that indicates you have a built-in audience for your book. Do you give speeches? Write a column? Have an e-mail newsletter? Do you appear on TV or radio? Have you been written about in newspapers?

Do you have a special degree? Any special awards? What organizations do you belong to?

Don't write this like a resume. Instead, write an informal biography. Remember, only include material related to your topic.

8) FORMAT

What will your book look like when it's published? Describe it here.

How many words will it be? (A double-spaced manuscript page contains 250 words.) How long it will take you to finish? (Take your best guess and then add three months.) What format do you want it to be published in—hardcover, trade paperback, or mass market paperback? Will there be any drawings or photographs? How many? In color or black and white? Will you have sidebars, checklists, quizzes, exercises or case studies? Will they be in every chapter?

9) PROMOTION STRATEGIES

Publishers need to be convinced that your book will sell. Tell them how you will make that happen. If you are a paid speaker, mention how many speeches you will give in the next year, and preferably where. List media appearances you've made in the past and how many you expect to make to promote your book. Say how much you are willing to spend on a publicist and ask the publisher to match that amount. List articles you can write in trade journals, e-zines, etc. Show how you plan on getting your book in front of the specific target audiences you mention earlier in the proposal.

10) OUTLINE

The outline proves you have enough to say to fill a book. Make it look like a table of contents minus the page numbers. Indicate Part I, Part II, etc., and individual chapter titles. List the headlines that will fall within each chapter as well. Write catchy, clever, funny, or evocative chapter titles and headings, if possible and appropriate. (At your bookstore, look at other books on the same shelf yours will be on to see how they handle this.)

Make sure your catchy chapter titles are understandable. You may want to add a second part that explains what they mean. For example, in a women's clothing book, instead of just using "In Sheep's Clothes" as the name of a chapter, make it "In Sheep's Clothes—Looking Better in a Sweater".

11) Chapter Summaries

Build even more evidence that you have a whole book, not just a long magazine article. Briefly describe the material you will include in each chapter for at least half a page, but no more than a full page. In each summary, mention the benefits the reader will receive. A good strategy is to talk to the reader directly, referring to her as "you".

Do everything you can to keep this interesting and emotional. If you have any short anecdotes, include them, or at least summarize them here.

Show editors and agents how organized your thinking is and how passionate you are about your topic, too.

12) Sample Chapters

What do agents and editors want to see in your sample chapters? Your knowledge, your heart, your personality and your writing skill.

Pick chapters that involve the meat of your topic. (If you're writing a book on make-up, showcase the chapter on lipstick, not the one on your special skincare diet.)

Choose one chapter that includes your most compelling story—one that evokes tears, laughter, or a feeling of "I've been there". For your second chapter, select the one that offers your best advice. If you're writing an autobiography, pick two chapters that create two different emotional moods.

Make the beginning of each chapter enticing. End each chapter in a way that leaves the reader curious about what comes next.

13) Appendix

Your press clippings, published writing, brochures and testimonials from clients belong here.

Enclose video of your greatest television appearance or of your best speech if it makes you appear telegenic. A cassette of your best radio interview can go along with your proposal if you are emphasizing radio in your promotion section.

Put these ingredients together in a bottle, shake vigorously, and you have the secret formula that has been selling books for decades.

Now let's look at these topics in depth.

CHAPTER 15

WIN THE TITLE GAME

Having a spectacular title for your book is like being seven feet tall when you try out for the high school basketball team. You start off with a huge advantage.

Susan Page, author of *The Shortest Distance between You and a Published Book,* says that "an extraordinary, show-stopping title" is essential to landing a six-figure book advance.

Why? Because agents and editors know that there are thousands of books vying for attention when you go to the bookstore.

A title is a book's headline. Its job is to persuade you to reach out and pull a book off the shelf and read the book jacket, instead of moving on to the next title.

Advertising executives have been studying headlines for almost a hundred years. John Caples, author of the classic book *Tested Advertising Methods*, says that "there are four important qualities which a headline may possess." They are:

1) Self-interest
2) News
3) Curiosity
4) Quick, easy way

In bookstores, these same principles apply. Readers are on the lookout for books with titles that offer a solution to their problems, appeal to their curiosity, or give them a quick, easy way to do something. (News is less of a factor in a bookstore.)

If your title grabs the attention of a casual reader, it will grab the attention of agents and editors as well.

WANT YOUR TITLE TO BE THE BEST? TAKE THE M-N-O-P-Q-R-S TEST!

The M-N-O-P-Q-R-S Test is a comprehensive list of methods that can be used to create effective, and sometimes show-stopping titles.

Every great title uses at least one of these techniques. Combining two usually makes a title outstanding.

M IS FOR METAPHOR

Want a great way to inspire a reader's curiosity and to differentiate your book? Use a metaphor in your title.

Here's how powerful is a great metaphor in your title can be:

One of the bestselling books on the differences in how men and women communicate is *You Just Don't Understand*, by Deborah Tannen. This book spent almost four years on the New York Times bestseller list. It is unquestionably a grand success.

But if Tannen had used a metaphor for her title, instead of a familiar statement from the vernacular, she might have created a cultural phenomenon like John Gray's *Men are From Mars, Women are From Venus*.

Though there is a difference in the content and style of these books, they cover similar ground and appeal to the same audience. But Gray's book is clearly the winner when it comes to commercial success. It has spawned at least five additional volumes, a game, seminars, and counseling centers. His title is permanently imprinted on the mind of an entire generation.

Want another example of a successful of a mega-success with a metaphor title? The *Chicken Soup for the Soul* series, as mentioned earlier, has sold more than 82 million books and has spawned somewhat successful imitators offering *A Cup of Comfort, Hot Chocolate,* and *Taste Berries* for a mothers, mystics, and a wide assortment of other souls.

FINDING YOUR METAPHOR

There are many ways to come up with a metaphor for your title. One simple approach is to look at things you are passionate about in your own life. They may give you more than your title—you may wind up with an angle to use for your whole book.

That's what happened to Rich Fettke.

Fettke, a past president of the Professional and Personal Coaches Association, got an agent with his proposal for a book called *The Power of Partnership*. His agent sent it to nine large publishers and Fettke received nine rejections.

Since Fettke's mission was to get published by one of the majors, he went back to the drawing board.

A little while later, Fettke was giving a speech in Dallas where his agent lives. They went out for drinks and dinner.

"I started telling him some of my stories, like when I was bungee jumping off the Golden Gate Bridge, and this close call skydive that became the opening for my book, and he said 'how come this is not in your book proposal?' And I just figured, 'why?'

And he said, 'This is really who you are. It's exciting and you relate so many things to it. It makes you come alive.' So I went back to the drawing board, recreated another proposal, and it was called *Extreme Success*. That was a complete turnaround."

Eight New York publishers wanted Fettke to fly out to discuss his book. So he spent his birthday in 2001 meeting with publishers.

Comedian Jack E. Leonard once joked (to Ed Sullivan), "There's nothing wrong with you that reincarnation won't cure."

He could have said the same thing about Rich Fettke's first book proposal.

Simon & Schuster's Fireside imprint picked up Rich's book for an advance that was well into six figures.

Using extreme sports as a metaphor for many of life's situations was the key to Fettke's success. And the fact that it reflected one of his passions only helped. He says: "When I really tapped into who I am, what makes me come alive, and all that, that's when everything started to break wide open."

To see a book proposal that netted a first-time author over six figures, see the back of this book. Rich's proposal is there. You will completely understand why Simon & Schuster was willing to invest in his creation.

M Is Also For
"Make The Familiar Strange"

In *Synectics*, William J. J. Gordon says that one of the best ways to generate ideas is to "make the familiar strange".

It's certainly useful when you want to generate a title or a concept for a book.

Let's pretend you want to write a book about dating.

How do you make the subject of dating 'strange'?

Myreah Moore found a way. She tells women to forget the rules and take the opposite approach to the opposite sex. Her title: *Date Like a Man: What men know about dating and are afraid you'll find out.*

That certainly takes dating in the something familiar way and makes it strange.

Moore's subtitle, by the way, comes from an old advertising fill-in-the-blank:

What _____ know about _____ and are afraid you'll find out.

Just fill in those blanks and you'll have a title or subtitle that automatically makes the familiar strange. This phrase says that some special group that you're not part of has a secret advantage in getting what they want.

For example, if you use "successful authors" for the first blank and "getting published" for the second you get:

What Successful Authors Know About Getting Published and are Afraid You'll Find Out!

Want to write a book about the stock market? Take **Short-Sellers** (folks who make money when a stock goes down) for the first blank and **the Stock Market** for the second:

What Short-Sellers Know About the Stock Market and are Afraid You'll Find Out!

Ronda Rich uses a more generous variation of this template, which implies that the special group is willing to share their knowledge. Here's the formula:

What _____ Know (About _____) That _____ Should

"About _____ " is in parentheses because it's optional.

The title of her book is:

What Southern Women Know (that Every Woman Should): Timeless Secrets to Get Everything You Want in Love, Life and Work.

Apply this formula and any special quality or interest you have can serve as a theme for your book—your ethnicity, your job, your hobbies, or even your personality.

Some titles may work better with a slightly different ending.

Here are a few I came up with:

> What *Bad Boys* Know About *Women* (That *Nice Guys* Should)
> What *Poker Players* Know (That Every *Negotiator* Should)
> What *Jewish Mothers* Know About Children (That Every Parent Should)

Of course, you don't have to use the obvious connections. Jewish mothers know about more than just raising kids. Think about filling the blanks in other ways. What else do Jewish mothers know about?

Try this:

> What *Jewish Mothers* Know About *Persuasion* (That Every *Sales Pro* Should)

You can also think outside the box and pick random nouns and try to relate them to your subject.

For example, dogs.

What can you come up with?

> What *Dogs* Know About *Hierarchy* (That Every *Manager* Should)

That isn't bad. A specific breed of dog would make it better:

> What *Pit Bulls* Know About *Hierarchy* (That Every *Manager* Should)

You don't have to actually use one of these titles to benefit from this exercise. The point is to get your brain to turn something familiar into something strange. **The titles** you create by filling in the blanks **may be more of a point of departure than a title you actually use.**

When you have a title like the ones listed above, continue its theme throughout your book proposal. Ms. Rich milks her Southern Woman concept with chapters such as:

It's More Than The Drawl, Y'all

Charm That Disarms

If Life Were Fair, Pecan Pie Would Have No Calories

N IS FOR NICHE

The secret behind niche marketing, and hence niche titles, is that everyone wants to buy something that's designed just for them.

When I look for suits, I go to the men's store that carries the largest number of suits in my size so I won't have to go to the trouble of having my pants hemmed.

People in bookstores look for a book that "suits" their particular needs.

Dan Poynter, the self-publishing guru, understands niche marketing. A client of his wrote about a special technique that allows working women to breastfeed. He wanted her to call her book *Breast Feeding for Working Women*. She didn't like that title. She said her system worked for all women.

Dan gave her a choice. 55% of new mothers go back to work. She could have 55% of the market to herself, or she could go after the whole pool of breastfeeding mothers and compete with twenty other authors.

Which would you choose?

When you're going after a niche market, it's essential that you mention your niche in the title of your book.

One of the most competitive places in a bookstore is the health and fitness section. Every celebrity and her personal trainer has their own workout book.

James Karas found a way to make his fitness book stand out. He targeted it to entrepreneurs and corporate managers. As a result, *The Business Plan for the Body* was a *New York Times* #1 Bestseller.

Karas uses more than his title to appeal to his target audience. Three headlines on the cover use language that makes them feel right at home:

"CRUNCH THE NUMBERS
FOR SUCCESSFUL WEIGHT LOSS

MANAGE YOUR METABOLISM
BY EATING THE RIGHT WAY

INVEST IN THE ONLY WORKOUT BOOK
YOU'LL EVER NEED"

The business metaphor successfully carves out a niche for this fitness book.

These three sentences mentioned above are the "hook" for this book. It's quite likely they were part of the Karas' book proposal.

The following line from his biography was probably in his proposal, too:

"Jim's clients shed pounds and shape up because they use a tried-and-true tool: the principals found in a classic business plan."

One other note: Karas was successful pitching this book because he is a credible expert on both fitness and business. He is a Wharton trained entrepreneur turned fitness professional with a number of clients who are CEOs. At one time he was also an accomplished private portfolio manager.

Another way to succeed in a competitive market is to move your book away from the competition. Mark Victor Hansen calls this "bypass marketing". *Buff Brides* by Sue Fleming, and *The Wedding Workout* by Tracy Effinger and Suzanne Rowen, both take this approach. You don't find these books in the crowded health and fitness section of your bookstore. Instead, they are shelved with the wedding books.

Great move, right? Instead of competing with a hundred fitness books, these books compete only with each other. And brides, who are always concerned about how they will look in their wedding gown, can grab one of these workout books along with the other books they need for their wedding.

N IS ALSO FOR NEGATIVE

A bookstore is a world of positive, sappy prescriptions for falling in love, having great sex, getting rich and thin and then playing better golf on your perfect vacation.

A simple way to distinguish your book from the competition is to have a negative title.

That's how F. J. Lennon's *Every Mistake in the Book: A Business How-Not-To* grabbed my attention.

I was compelled to look at it. I wanted to make sure I wasn't making any of those mistakes!

Dr. Laura Schlessinger has an entire series of bestsellers with negative titles:

10 Stupid Things Women Do To Mess Up Their Lives
10 Stupid Things Men Do To Mess Up Their Lives
10 Stupid Things Couples Do To Mess Up Their Relationships
Stupid Things Parents Do To Mess Up Their Kids

Think about turning your how-to book into a how-not-to. It might give you an approach that will help your book sell.

O IS FOR OPPOSITES

Something in our brains that makes us respond favorably to the use of opposites. Randy Peyser uses them in both the title and the subtitle of *Crappy to Happy: Small Steps to Big Happiness NOW!*

This is also a memorable title because it's short, it rhymes, and it uses slightly impolite language.

Opposites can also help you create an angle for your book. Robert Kiyosaki used opposites to create the entire *Rich Dad, Poor Dad* series.

You don't even have to use words or concepts that are exact opposites.

The Power of Losing Control is still a satisfying title, even though power and losing control are not technically antonyms. Our brains "round off" the concept to make it work.

P IS FOR PUN

Here's how you create a title with a pun in it: Take two subjects and make a list of words that relate to each. Then see if they have a word in common. Once you find that word, search your brain for phrases that include it.

Pretend you're writing the life story of a manager of a baseball team who left baseball to become the conductor of an opera company.

To come up with a pun, make a list of baseball words:

Baseball
Bats
Gloves
Bases

Then make a list of opera words:

Opera
Arias
Tenors
Basses

Check to see if they have anything in common..

Baseball	Opera
Bats	Arias
Gloves	Tenors
Bases	Basses

Baseball has "Bases" and opera has "Basses", (the guys with really deep voices). Though these words are spelled differently, they share the same pronunciation.

Next, think of common expressions with the word "bases" in them. Then convert the word "bases" to "basses". For example:

Rounding the Basses
Covering All Your Basses
The Basses Are Loaded
Running The Basses

The last two titles could work well. Make sure you add an explanatory subtitle. For example:

Running the Basses: My Life, Or How I Went From Playing the Mets to Playing at the Met

My favorite title with a pun in it? Peggy Klaus's *Brag: The Art of Tooting Your Own Horn Without Blowing It.*

P IS ALSO FOR PROMISE AND PRESCRIPTION

The difference between a promise and a prescription is that a prescription has a specific amount of something or a time frame attached to it. Of all the titles you see in your bookstore, promises and prescriptions are the most common.

The quick, easy way headlines that John Caples talks about fall into this category. Every how-to book falls into it, too.

Write a Book Without Lifting a Finger makes a promise that you will learn to write a book without much work.

The title of this section, *Land a Book Deal From Just Twenty Pages*, is a prescription. It is a step-by-step guide to getting published. Instead of making a promise based on time, however, it makes one based on the number of pages you will have to write.

When it comes to selling your book, prescriptions are stronger than promises. Publishers have even given a name to this category of books: prescriptive non-fiction.

Q IS FOR QUESTION

Why do questions work as titles? One reason is that they are uncommon, like negative titles. Also, the best question titles express what's going on in the minds of a book's target audience.

Susan Page titled her book with a question many single people ask: *If I'm So Wonderful, Why Am I Still Single?*

Les Charles picked another common question: *Why is Everybody So Cranky?*

As mentioned above, if a title doesn't explain what a book is about, a subtitle must be used. Ms. Charles added this subtitle: *The Ten Trends Complicating Our Lives and What We Can Do About Them.*

Lou Gerstner, former chairman of IBM went even further with his title. *Who Says Elephants Can't Dance?* is a question that employs a metaphor. As mentioned above, using more than one of these techniques at the same time will give you a better title.

It also is an answer to a famous quote that Gerstner was undoubtedly aware of when he chose his title. When Gary Moss spoke about the decline of the large advertising agencies' monopoly in marketing in *Forbes* magazine, he said, "You can teach an elephant to dance, but the likelihood of it stepping on your toes is very high."

R IS FOR RHYME & REPETITION

Rhyme in your title, particularly if your title is short, makes it both delightful and memorable. Two people who knew I was working on this book mentioned *Crappy to Happy* to me as soon as it came out.

One of my favorite recent titles is *Niche and Grow Rich*, by Jennifer Basye Sander and Peter Sander. It rhymes, it's short, and it makes reference to another bestselling title--*Think and Grow Rich* by Napoleon Hill.

(That's another title technique that will be described in just a moment.)

As a songwriter, I learned that rhyme also speeds up a long line. It does the same thing for a long title or subtitle. *Knitting With Dog Hair* has an incredibly long, but wonderful subtitle: ***Better*** *a **Sweater** from a Dog You Know and Love than from a **Sheep** You'll Never **Meet**.*

The rhymes make it go faster.

Repetition is like rhyme. It appeals to the brain and helps you remember a title. *Change Your Brain, Change Your Life* is a title that both repeats words and offers a promise.

Why Men Stay, Why Men Stray adds rhyme to the equation.

R IS ALSO FOR REFERENCE

Many books use a title that makes reference to the title of another successful book, song or movie. *Niche and Grow Rich* has already been mentioned. Here are a few other variations on successful titles:

Women Who Think Too Much
Food and Loathing
50 Ways to Read Your Lover

S IS FOR STATEMENT

Another title strategy is to take a statement from a story you tell. It needs to be a sentence that everyone understands and preferably will be one that gives people an emotional reaction.

For example, many people asked Betty Rollins what she did when she first found out she had breast cancer. Her answer, *First, You Cry*, became the title of her book.

Another approach is to use statements that are common expressions, such as:

Don't Sweat the Small Stuff
Get With the Program
Mom, They're Teasing Me

A LAST WORD ON TITLES

The value of a great title can't be over-emphasized. Copywriters say to spend 90% of your time on the headline in order to make an advertisement a success.

You can't spend that percentage of your writing time on your book's title, but you can spend a few minutes trying to improve it every day until you have one that will leave readers, editors and agents salivating.

Copywriters have another strategy worth borrowing. They test their headlines.

Make a list of possible titles and ask twenty people to tell you their first and second choices for the title of your book. The one that gets picked the most is the title you should pick.

CREATING YOUR TITLE PAGE

To complete the title page, type the title and subtitle of your book in the center of the page.

Add your contact information below that. Include your snail mail address, your voice, fax and cell phone numbers, and your e-mail address.

Simple Housekeeping Rules

Before we move on to the next chapter, there are some simple housekeeping measures to remember as you put together a proposal:

- Your book proposal needs its own table of contents. That comes right after any endorsements you may have. Either wait until your final draft is finished to create it, or you can make it as you go along. Add page numbers at the very end when you've completed the final draft of your proposal. This way you won't have to change them all the time.
- Agents and editors expect submitted manuscripts to be double-spaced. This makes them easier to read and edit.

CHAPTER 16

PUT 'EM IN THE MOOD

Unless you are an unrepentant fan, Oprah Winfrey knows she has to grab your attention at the top of her show. That's why each episode starts with an overview: two or three of the most dramatic moments, followed by information about people who are in the same boat.

At the start of your proposal, you have to grab an agent or editor's attention in the same way.

You want to get them rooting for you.

When I was a headhunter, I would sometimes make a quick decision from just a conversation with someone or a portion of his resume. If he said or wrote the right thing, I would begin to root for him.

Once I started rooting for him, I would look for ways to justify my attitude. Where his skills were weak, I would see it as something that could be easily overcome. Where his ability was average, I would think, 'well, at least he knows enough to get the job done'. And where his work showed some talent, I would think of him as a superstar.

I know that I am not the only one deluding myself in this way. It's human nature. People look for ways to justify their first impressions.

Naturally, agents and editors do the same thing. When your book proposal makes a good first impression with them, they want you to succeed.

Rebecca Saletan, editor at Farrar, Straus & Giroud says that people have certain misconceptions about an editor's life:

> " . . . they think we sit here surrounded by masterpieces, trying to decide which of them to publish. We don't. We sit surrounded by masses of not-very-good writing and stuff that's just okay. I'm looking for something that absolutely captivates me."[4]

To captivate publishing pros, start with a good overview. When they like your overview, they will root for you even if there are weaknesses in your proposal.

STEP 1: GIVE 'EM THE HOOK

The first two or three sentences of the overview is called the hook. It's where you grab the reader's attention. Here are some techniques to help you create one:

---

[4] Quoted in *Book Editors Talk to Writers,* by Judy Mandell

1) **Startle your reader with a stunning statistic.** For example, "Over 25 million women over forty wake up exhausted every morning through no fault of their own. They do everything right—balancing work and play, delegating household tasks, and taking an appropriate amount of time for themselves. These women have made only one mistake: they share their life and their bed with a man who snores. *One Love, Two Bedrooms* is written for them."

2) **Talk about a common problem.** Here is how Cindy Ventrice starts her proposal for *Make Their Day*: "Most employee recognition is a dismal failure that leaves peak performers feeling inadequately recognized. Organizations set up costly and ineffective recognition programs that try to buy employee loyalty and performance. Individual managers make erroneous assumptions about what employees want. When recognition efforts fail, managers say that recognition doesn't work."

3) **Tell a good story.** Usually, a *short* story works best. But if you have a story that a) is incredibly moving, funny, dramatic, exciting, or shows spectacular results and b) would be appropriate as the actual beginning of your book, then follow in Rich Fettke's footsteps and take as much time as you need. Rich's story takes six hundred words at the beginning of his proposal. It also became the beginning of his book. Here's how it begins:

> "I was ready to push my limits, to succeed at something I had never done before. That meant boarding the waiting airplane and pushing myself through a cargo door while cruising at 90 mph at 14,000 feet.
>
> I stood at this brink for one reason: I wanted to break through the unfounded terror I had about doing a solo skydive out of an airplane."

4) **Use a spectacular simile or magnificent metaphor.** Peggy Vincent sold her memoirs about her experiences as a midwife for over $100,000. Felicia Eth, her agent, gives out Peggy's book proposal as an example to study. Here is the paragraph Peggy starts with:

> "The first time I saw a baby born, it was more magical to me than seeing a white dove fly free from the hands of a sorcerer – more magical because it wasn't magic. It was real. Since that day in 1962, I have nourished myself by tapping into the passion of women giving birth."

The rest of Peggy's proposal is in the back of this book.

5) **Ask questions that make the reader say yes.** Start off with three questions that make the reader say, 'yes, I am one of the people who needs this book.' Here's how Kenneth Christian hooks readers:

"Are you stuck in a job you don't love? Are you always putting off decisions? Are you reluctant to challenge yourself? If so, you may be *Your Own Worst Enemy.*"

For more examples of hooks, go to literary agent James Levine's website, http://www.levinegreenberg.com. Just click on the word "CATEGORIES" on the left, then select one of the categories that come up. You'll be able to surf through descriptions of all the books his agency represents in that category. These short descriptions are hooks.

STEP 1A: IF NECESSARY, EXPAND

If you haven't fully explained who your audience is and what your book will solve for them or offer them in your hook, continue for another paragraph or two.

Think about your readers and ask yourself these questions:

Who are they and why will they read your book?

Do they have a physical or emotional need that your book will solve?

Is there a problem they need to fix for themselves or for the world?

Do they need to escape, or feel, or laugh, or be up-to-date?

Do they have a significant problem or desire for their business or their finances?

Are they part of a particular group that this problem affects?

Why is this problem important to them?

STEP 2: INTRODUCE THE CURE

Now tell how your book solves the problems you mentioned above. List your book's *features* (subjects, exercises, diagrams, photos) and what *benefits* those features will provide.

You can use a bulleted list here, just as you would on the back of a book.

This section needs to read like jacket copy. Here's an example from the back cover of Rhonda Abrams' *The Successful Business Plan.* It's an excellent example of how this part of the overview should be written. I've put the **benefits in bold** and underlined the features.

"[*The Successful Business Plan*] is a **step-by-step guide** to a more fulfilling business [that includes:]

- 183 tips from 16 insiders reveal[ing] what most **impresses the people who evaluate and fund business plans**
- 99 worksheets [that] cover all critical plan sections to **get you started fast**
- How to put your facts and figures into a **compelling, readable story**
- [A] sample business plan . . . written in the accepted wording and style, **providing an excellent model**
- Special chapters for service, manufacturing, retail and Internet companies

- The Abrams Method of Flow-Through Financials [to help you] **easily complete your financial projections**—even if you're a financial novice
- Winning tips for competitions."

One last word: Make sure the entire overview is consistent in how it addresses the audience of the book. If you mention readers, then use "readers", "they" and "them" to refer to readers, and not "you".

Conversely, if you are using the second person, or "you" to refer to readers, make sure you use "you" and "yours" throughout the overview and not "readers."

STEP 3: ANYTHING THEY CAN DO, YOU CAN DO BETTER

On the Jewish holiday of Passover, the youngest son is asked to recite four questions. The first question is "Why is this night different from all other nights?" The child then explains that on all other nights we eat sitting straight up, and on this night we lean while we eat; on all other nights we eat bread that has risen, on this night we eat matzoh (unleavened bread), etc.

That's your next task. Explain why your book is different from all other books on your topic.

Here's how Cindy Ventrice did it for her book:

> "There are no publications that compete directly with the proposed book. There are many books that focus on rewards without delving into the underlying issues of recognition. No publication:
>
> - Emphasizes the importance of individualizing recognition for each employee.
> - Examines the role of every individual in creating high-impact recognition.
> - Focuses on the role of relationship in recognition."

STEP 4: SHOW 'EM WHY YOU'RE THE ONE TO DO IT

If you have been promised any endorsements, include a short paragraph like this one by Peggy Vincent:

> "Suzanne Arms, filmmaker, international childbirth advocate, and author of the pivotal Immaculate Deception, will write the foreword. The following authors, all of whom have read material, have agreed to provide endorsements:"

Then list the authors and one or two of their biggest credits.

The next paragraph is a brief biography. Explain why you're qualified to write this particular book. You can save any other information for your full biography later in the proposal. Here's what Peggy included in her overview:

"My years of hospital experience prior to the takeover of obstetrics by high-tech machines, as well as my 15 years attending home births, allow me to straddle the dichotomy that exists between the medical model of birth with its focus on the science of childbirth, and the midwifery model, which pays equal heed to the artistry of birth. In **_Baby Catcher_**, as well as in my midwifery practice, I find it easy to balance the conflicts that often separate these ideologies."

STEP 5: WHAT'S IT LOOK LIKE TO YOU?

Describe the format of your book in this next paragraph, which closes your overview. If you have a legitimate reason why your book should be released as a hardcover book instead of a trade paperback, mention it here. Otherwise, just estimate your word count (each double-spaced page is 250 words), how much of your book is already finished, and mention any illustrations or photographs that are to be included.

Diane Dreher did it this way:

"*Inner Gardening* will be approximately 250 manuscript pages or 60,000-80,000 words, about the same length as Diane's most recent book, *The Tao of Womanhood*. Diane will provide a copy of the USDA Plant Hardiness Zone Map and appropriate illustrations for each of the five sections."

CHAPTER 17

MARKETING MATTERS

The next two sections of a proposal deal with the market for your book. They expand on what you wrote in the overview *The Audience* discusses who will buy your book. *The Competition* shows that it will deliver something new.

Your research in these areas may further define the content of your book.

Independent publishing guru Jerrold Jenkins, in his book *Publish to Win,* says potential promotional angles should affect what you write about:

> "A book on coping with the holidays, for example, could appeal to a wide range of readers with the right planning. One chapter might be devoted to gay issues during the holidays, another dealing with alcoholic relatives, still another with coping with infertility during the holidays. These three different chapters provide three different slants for media coverage or entire reprints in specific magazines."

Researching the competition may also impact your material. You may decide a topic that gets just one page in another book deserves a whole chapter in yours.

THE AUDIENCE

Is there a market for your book? This section is where you prove it.

Show publishers who will buy your book.

The usual format for this section is a bulleted list.

First, mention any books on a topic similar to yours that have sold well. If you don't already know about these books, you can find out about them by searching at Amazon.com for similarly themed books. (If a book ranks in the top 5,000 at Amazon, it's worth mentioning.)

Allan Klein, in his proposal for *The Courage to Laugh,* wrote this:

> "Who will buy this book? . . . The general public whose interest in the once-taboo topic of death and dying themes has already been established by past successes of such books as Elisabeth Kubler-Ross' *On Death and Dying* and, more recently, Sherwin Nuland's *How We Die.* (The latter was on the *New York Times* bestseller list in both hardcover and paperback for 25 weeks.)"

Allan's proposal is in the back of this book.

Continue by listing current events, trends, or major articles in national, high circulation periodicals that your topic is related to. Mention any tie-ins between your book and the latest news. If there is a trend mentioned in the media, or a hot new television show, explain how your book relates to that. List any recent mentions in Time, Newsweek, the New York Times, the Washington Post, USA Today or the Wall Street Journal.

Next, describe specific groups that will have a particular interest in your subject matter, starting with the largest first. When possible, describe who they are, what they want, and what benefit they will receive from your book. Use statistics. *Be very specific. And mention every group that applies.* (The bigger your audience, the bigger potential for your advance.)

Here are several kinds of groups:

- **Identifiable Demographic Groups,** such as divorced women over 40, children with A.D.D., couples getting married for the second time, people who are self-employed
- **People who watch specific channels, television shows, or movies**, such as viewers of ESPN 2, the Sci-Fi Channel, *Crossing Over with John Edward*, or movie, *The Buena Vista Social Club*. Use this statistic to identify a narrower group than the broad audience that watches *C.S.I.* or *Friends*.
- **People who subscribe to particular magazines**. If you are writing a book about planning a wedding, list each of the half a dozen or so bridal magazines and their circulations individually, then note the total numbers of subscribers.
- **Organizations and associations that have a reason to be interested in your topic**. List each of these organizations individually.
- **Friends and relatives of the people who are involved with your topic.** Mention them if you are writing a proposal that deals with physical or mental conditions.

FINDING STATISTICS

Here's how to find the statistics you will need:

- Look at U.S. Census figures at http://www.census.gov
- Search the web using the name of the group you are looking for and the word "statistics" as one of your search terms; other possible terms that may be useful are "percentage", and "by age".
- Go to the library and look at the Standard Periodical Directory, which lists magazines and their circulations
- The Encyclopedia of Associations is also at the library. This will help you find organizations and associations that are interested in your topic.
- Ask the librarian at the nearest university for help.

If you can't find what you want on your own, Google has a new service called Google Answers where you can bid to get help from researchers with expertise in online searching. Bids range from $2.50 to $200.00. If you are looking for a small amount of information, $10 or $20 should do the trick.

They also tell you what they did so you can use their technique next time. I was very satisfied with the service they provided for a $20 bid. They are at: http://answers.google.com/answers/main.

If even that doesn't work for you, try calling the professional researchers who advertise in the back of Writer's Digest magazine.

PUT IT ALL TOGETHER

Every piece of your book proposal is a showcase for your writing talent (or that of your ghostwriter). Though a straight factual presentation of who your audience is won't hurt your chances of getting published, a proposal with a more exciting presentation will add to your credibility as a writer. A beautifully written proposal helps you get a bigger advance.

Rich Fettke's description of the market for *Extreme Success* makes a topic that could have been dull sound exciting:

> "The strongest target group for **Extreme Success** is made up of young business people with strong entrepreneurial spirit and an intense desire to achieve high profile success at work. At the same time, they seek fulfilling personal lives. Hungry for "success secrets," they search for valuable information in books, at programs and seminars and on the Internet. As industry mavericks that drive change, extreme achievers often run their own companies or work for an aggressive corporation where they are responsible for their own business development. They aim to scale the corporate ladder as quickly as possible before jumping over to another company for higher pay, more generous benefits and greater recognition."

THE COMPETITION

The next section of a proposal deals with the competition. See the proposals at the end of this book for examples.

No matter what the subject, no author covers it perfectly. Writers focus on the parts of a topic they're interested in and are good at. They'll make only passing reference to those areas they find less compelling. Their books mirror their own strengths and weaknesses.

I found this to be true when I looked through the literature on how to write a book proposal. A book I admire, with a hard to remember title, was impressive in all areas—except how to create a strong title.

Another book I like has very little to offer on how to write the promotion section of a book proposal. This mirrors the author's own lack of interest in promotion. At last count, he's made 12 radio appearances plus one on TV to promote his amazing output of sixty books. This is less promotion than most authors do for one book, let alone sixty.

Readers have widely different mindsets, too. A thorough, step-by-step how-to book will be too detailed for a reader who likes quick, easy to read information. Another reader who wants all the information possible will complain when a book isn't detailed enough.

That's why there's room for *your* book.

The competitive analysis in a proposal lets you say what your book does better than everyone else's.

If this makes you nervous, think how lucky you are that you're not writing a book on English grammar. Imagine trying to separate your book on a topic where nothing changes.

Nonetheless, here at my Borders bookstore in little Santa Cruz, (population: 50,000) there are twenty different grammar titles. That doesn't include the grammar books for folks who speak English as a second language.

Here's a quick and dirty description of five of these books. Notice how each one is different from the others:

The Elements of Style -- short and to the point, a classic, academic style

Nitty Gritty Grammar – short, fun to read, lots of cartoons

Painless Grammar – fun, cartoons, with exercises so you can practice

Grammar 101 – modern, to the point, no illustrations or fluff, just facts

A Grammar Book for You and I, Oops Me – long (430 pages!) with interesting stories on the history behind the rules of grammar

Though these books share the same basic purpose—to teach grammar—each of them is different. They each take a distinctive approach that appeals to readers with different needs.

The competition section shows that your book brings a unique spin to your topic.

Mention each book that will compete with yours. Describe in detail what your book does that no other book on the subject succeeds at.

This section helps agents and editors look good when they pitch your book.

You already know agents sell books to editors. But editors have to sell your book, too. Each publishing house has an editorial board that meets as a group to decide whether or not to buy a book. This board is made up of other editors and people from the marketing department.

The last thing an editor wants to have happen after she makes a big sales pitch for your book is for one of the marketing people pipe up that there is a book just like yours that is already out.

If you've mentioned this book in your competition analysis, your editor will have the ammunition she needs to explain how your book is different. If you haven't mentioned it, then she looks bad.

You are probably aware of which books compete with yours. You may not know all of them, however. So do a search on your topic at Amazon.com. Find the five or six highest ranked books closest to yours in subject matter.

No need to mention any books that are out of print. But make sure you cover any books listed on Amazon that are due out in the next few months.

Start this section with a summary of what your book covers that no other book does.

Then, one at a time, list the title, the author, the publisher, and the year each competing book was published. If the book was revised, mention the last year it was revised instead of the year of publication.

Give a brief description of what the book does well and describe how your book is better or different. Mention any topics your book includes that the other book leaves out.

Then continue to the next book, and the next one, etc. You may find yourself repeating the same information again and again. That's acceptable in this section.

Here's a short sample from Allan Klein's proposal:

> "At this time, there is a great deal of interest in books pertaining to humor and books dealing with death but little, if any, competition for *The Courage to Laugh* which examines both of these subjects.

> *Love, Medicine & Miracles* by Bernie Siegel (Harper Perennial, revised 1990). This book explored how "exceptional cancer patients" take control of their situation. Humor is mentioned as one coping and healing tool but the main focus of this book is on other ways that cancer patients deal with their illness."

One final note: Don't limit your comparison to content. Take a lesson from the grammar books above and mention how your book differs from others in terms of style, too.

CHAPTER 18

WHO ARE YOU
AND HOW WILL PEOPLE FIND OUT?

The next three sections of a book proposal include your bio, the format of your book, and how you plan to promote your book.

ABOUT THE AUTHOR

This is where you write your bio.

Want some professional advice? Literary agent James Levine tells potential clients not to be shy. "Err on the side of tooting your own horn too loudly," he says. "We'll help you tone it down if necessary."

Your task: Make a brilliant case that you are an expert on your topic. Mention anything and everything that that will help you prove that. Don't be formal; be conversational, without being cute. Agents want to see that you are truly qualified to write this book. Here's a checklist:

✓ Are you qualified because of the work you do?
✓ Do you have articles published on this subject?
✓ Have you received any awards?
✓ Any special degrees?

Emphasize anything that shows you have a built-in audience:

✓ Do you give speeches or workshops? How many people have seen you speak over the years? Use this format: "I have given speeches and workshops to over 25,000 people since 1999."
✓ Do you write a column? What is the combined circulation of the periodicals in which it appears?
✓ Do you have your own newsletter or e-zine? How many subscribers does it reach?
✓ Have you been a guest on television? List your appearances. If you've been on more than four or five shows, list the highlights and the total number.
✓ Been interviewed on radio? Mention the highlights and the number of shows.
✓ Have you been the subject of or quoted in articles? Mention any national publications.

Finally, bring up any articles or books you have published that are not related to your topic. This gives you additional credibility as a writer.

When It's Personal

You may have qualifications that come from personal experience. Allen Klein handles this with a special bullet point labeled "Why I am the one to write this book." Underneath it he writes:

"The desire to write *The Courage to Laugh* emerged from a lesson I learned during my wife's terminal illness. Because of her keen sense of humor, she showed me that laughter can ease pain, lift us above our upsets, and soften our suffering. In other words, when we are in pain and wish that something would "take us away from it all," humor does exactly that.

This experience of losing a loved one, along with my former and current careers, plays a major role in this book and makes me the ideal person to write it."

Two Ways To Boost Your Credibility

Sometimes you need some extra oomph to convince a publisher that you're the one to write a book. Here are two ways to do that:

1) **Find someone with great credentials to write a foreword for you.** It's always good to have someone well known write a foreword to your book. But in a case where your qualifications are not as strong as they might be, this is essential. Their credibility adds to yours, making it easier for you to sell your book to publishers, and to the general public.

For instance, let's say you wrote a screenplay that got made but went straight to video. Though you have a certain amount of experience, it may not be enough to persuade anyone that you are especially qualified to write a book on film criticism. But if you could get Roger Ebert to write the foreword, or even agree to write a blurb for the cover of your book, you would now add his credibility to yours.

You wouldn't even have to find someone as famous as Ebert. You could seek out a critic or a university professor who has a national reputation with film buffs, but not the general public. Or you could approach a critic from a newspaper in one of the twenty-five largest cities in the U. S.

2) **Look for someone with better qualifications in your field to collaborate with you.** This might not be your ideal solution. But if you are not an expert in your own right on a particular subject, teaming up with someone who is may be what gets you published.

Laura Davis is the author of a bestselling book about surviving incest. Her interviews with families of incest survivors and her experiences as a parent herself led her to an idea for a book on parenting. But her only official credential was that she was the parent of one child who was only two years old. That wasn't enough experience to pass media scrutiny as an expert on children of all ages.

Janis Keyser was a child development educator for twenty years and the parent of three grown children. But she was not very well known outside of Santa Cruz. It's difficult to sell books on parenting, because every parent in the world thinks they are qualified to write one. Without a national following, Janis was going to have a hard time selling a parenting book on her own.

So Laura and Janis teamed up and wrote *Becoming the Parent You Want to Be*, which was published by Broadway Books, an imprint of Random House. Keyser gave Davis the parenting credibility she lacked. Davis lent Keyser name recognition.

They both developed better credentials from writing together. Davis, having written a book on parenting, has the credentials to write about parenting on her own now. Keyser has a successful book that has built her the national audience she previously lacked.

All in all, it was a fruitful pairing.

FORMAT

The next part of a proposal is a small section where you describe what your book will look like when it is finished.

Start off with the outside of your book. What kind of picture is in your mind when you see it?

Is it a hardcover book, a trade paperback, or a mass-market paperback (the kind you find on the racks of the grocery stores)?

Is it a standard size, or is it different? There is a big market for smaller, shorter books, such as *Fish, Don't Sweat the Small Stuff* and *If Life is a Game*.

Describe the physical properties of your book.

Next, move to the inside.

How many words will it be? The books mentioned above have fewer pages, and since they are smaller, they have fewer words per page than the other books in their categories.

To estimate based on the style of your book, a normal sized hardcover or trade paperback has between 300 and 400 words per page.

But there are also variations. The hardcover version of *The Christmas Box* only has about 125 words per page. The whole book is only about 15,000 words. Nonetheless, it was a bestseller.

To come up with the number of words you will be writing, multiply the number of pages you want to write by the number of words you expect to be on a page. (If you want to base your guess on the traditional, double-spaced manuscript page, each of those contains about 250 words. With that method, use the phrase "manuscript pages" when you describe the length of your book.[5]

Then estimate how long it will take you to finish the manuscript. Unless you are writing about something timely, always say that it will take you at least six months to finish writing the book. If publishers think it will take you less than six months, then they may offer you a smaller book advance. The logic behind this is that a book

---

[5] e.g. "This book will be approximately 350 manuscript pages."

advance is supposed to help you live until you finish your book. If it's already written, you have plenty of time for work.

Finally, discuss some of the features of the book. Will there be any drawings, cartoons or photographs? How many? In color or black and white? Will you have sidebars, checklists, quizzes, exercises or case studies? Will they be in every chapter?

For examples, see each of the proposals at the back of the book.

Promotion Strategies

Despite most people's romantic notions, the publishing industry is a business. Publishers need to know how and why your book will sell.

Hyperion President Robert Miller poses the question that publishers want you to answer with this section of the proposal: "How is anyone going to hear about this book? It's a valid question. Otherwise, if nobody hears about it, it is literally a tree falling in the forest."

Where To Start

In *Guerilla Marketing for Writers*, Michael Larsen says that every author's promotion plans should start with the following statement:

> "On signing the contract, the author will match the publisher's out-of-pocket consumer promotion budget up to $X."

Replace X with whatever you can afford.

This statement shows that you are committed to promoting your book out of your own pocket. It also commits the publisher to spending money on your book, too.

But if you say it, you better mean it, because publishers will add that phrase to your contract.

If you can hire a publicist, mention that next. Barbara Bartlein's book proposal includes this statement: "Ms. Bartlein will hire a publicist through Planned Television Arts."

Here are some publicists that specialize in book publicity:

Planned TV Arts
www.plannedtvarts.com
Contact Brian Feinblum
PH 212-583-2718
feinblumb@ruderfinn.com

Annie Jennings PR
www.anniejenningspr.com/
908.281.6201
Annie@AnnieJenningsPR.com

Radio And TV

Next, list radio and television shows you have already been on that you can be booked on again to promote your book.

If you haven't been on a particular show, but have a personal relationship with someone who works there and it would be appropriate for your topic, mention that.

Many authors advertise in RTIR (*Radio-Television Interview Reports*) to get radio stations to call for interviews. It is a magazine that goes out to 4000 radio stations. You can get a three-month ad for about $750. They say their average advertiser gets about fifteen appearances from that package. They are at http://www.rtir.com. If you plan to advertise in RTIR, mention how long you will be advertising in it.

Don't mention that your book would be perfect for Oprah, or anyone else, unless you have been on their show before.

Talks And Articles

Next, if you are willing to fund your own book tour (or already have contacts that will pay you for speeches), put together a list of cities where you will speak. These should primarily be in the top twenty-five markets.

Your list should include what you will do to get you or your book in front of members of trade organizations that have an interest in your topic.

If the members of some of these organizations can influence large numbers of people to recommend your book, mention this. Use numbers whenever possible. Peggy Vincent does a very good job of this in the marketing plan of her proposal for *Baby Catcher*.

Mention newspapers and magazines that have written about you that you can contact again to promote your book.

List any publications you can write articles for, including newsletters and e-zines. Also list any publications that may want to review your book.

Note any organizations you belong to with membership lists you can use for a mailing.

Specialty Markets

Are there specialty stores or catalogs that can carry your product? For example, if you are writing a wedding book, mention bridal shows, bridal shops, and florists as potential specialty markets. Make a heading called "Alternate Markets" and list these.

Where To Get More Ideas

If you need to brainstorm for additional ideas, here are some resources to check:

1) Get a subscription to Book Marketing Update at http://www.bookmarketingupdate.com. It costs $1 for a one-month trial subscription and you are given access to over sixty back issues, which

you can print out and keep, even if you decide not to continue your subscription, which is $19.95 per month. (You do have to call or e-mail them to cancel your subscription.)

Book Marketing Update has a tremendous amount of specific information about promoting your book to the media. It also offers "in-depth case histories of successful book marketing campaigns." Many of these campaigns include ideas that you will be able to use for your book.

2) Buy some of the following books. They each contain ideas that you can use in your book proposal:

- *1001 Ways To Market Your Book* by John Kremer. This is by the editor of Book Marketing Update.
- *Guerilla Marketing for Writers* by Jay Conrad Levinson, Rick Frishman and Michael Larsen. Levinson is the bestselling author of the *Guerilla Marketing* series, Frishman is the president of publicity firm Planned TV Arts and Larsen is an author and a top-notch agent.
- *Jump Start Your Book Sales* by Tom and Marilyn Ross. Married to each other, these keen promoters are two of the top marketers in self-publishing.
- *How To Publish and Promote Online* by M. J. Rose and Angela Adair-Hoy will give you inexpensive ideas you can use to promote your book on the net. Rose published her first novel on the net and got bought out by a major publisher and Adair-Hoy has a newsletter for writers that has 70,000 subscribers. She also owns Booklocker, a successful online publishing firm. If you want your proposal to include inexpensive promotion ideas that can be implemented online, this is a good book to get.

CHAPTER 19

BOOK MATTERS

The three remaining sections of your book proposal are about what goes inside your book. First up is the outline.

THE OUTLINE

The outline in your proposal should look like the Table of Contents to a published book, minus the page numbers. What you submit in your proposal won't be your final version, but it could be close.

There are a variety of ways to come up with an outline. Here's what I do:

1. First, I come up with a list of possible chapters. I then take each chapter and break it into sub-sections. I also make a guess as to how long each chapter will be.
2. I add up all the pages that I have guessed for each chapter. If there aren't enough pages, I work on ways to stretch the book out. For the hair color book I ghosted, we added a short chapter on skin care and one on diet and exercise. Not exactly about hair color, but justifiable. The segue we used was, "Now that you have such beautiful hair, you want to your skin to look good, too", etc.
3. Once I know I have enough material for a book, I figure out an order for the chapters.
4. Finally, I give the chapters and the sub-sections clever names.

TRICKS OF THE TRADE

Every book is different, so it's hard to come up with general rules. Here are some tidbits that might come in handy as you do your outline:

- Maury Yeston, the Tony-winning songwriter for the Broadway hits *Nine* and *Titanic* once taught me that to write a song, you say 'this is what you're gonna do', you do it, and then you say 'this is what I've done'. You can do the same thing with a book.
- Most books start off with an introduction or a chapter about why the author is writing the book.
- Many books are organized around a step-by-step process. The first chapter is an overview, then the rest of the chapters are the steps.

- Other books are organized by categories. Then you break each category down into sub-categories. Then you break each sub-category into three more.

    I once ghostwrote the proposal for a numerology book. (Numerology is like astrology except it uses the letters of your name and your birth date to make predictions.) Our introduction was why the numerologist wrote the book. Our first chapter was the math you needed to come up with the formulas. After that, we discussed the meaning of each number, one through nine, one number per chapter.

    To fatten up each chapter, we added sub-categories like the characteristics of a "number one" as a lover, as a teacher, as a parent, what their favorite gift was, etc.

- Other chapter extenders are quizzes, exercises, lists of Dos and Don'ts, graphs, charts, and case studies. You can also break each prescription into three levels: the least, the medium amount and the most.

- Author Marsha Yudkin recommends taking a bunch of index cards and writing topics that apply to the subject you are writing about. Once you have between fifty and a hundred of these, you put them in piles of related ideas. Each pile is one chapter.

- If your program contains seven to twenty-five principles, each principle can be a chapter.

- Scott Edelstein's *100 Things Every Writer Needs to Know* has one hundred chapters. Each chapter is two pages.

- If you are writing a book about the secrets of a dozen millionaires, it can be organized in two ways: you can have a separate chapter per millionaire or you can have chapters about central themes that each millionaire comments on.

- For an autobiography, start figuring out what your chapters will be by picking out the main events of your life. If you have enough main events, those are your chapters.

- Here are some broad questions that might help you come up with extra chapter ideas:
    o Why did you write this book? What's your story with regard to this topic?
    o What are the factors that stop people from doing what you suggest?
    o What can go wrong?
    o How do you fix that?
    o Are there groups of people that are especially affected by your subject? Can you give them each a chapter?
    o Once you change this area of your life, what else should you do?
    o Do you have a chapter on what not to do?
    o What about a chapter on what to do if you get really good at this? Can your reader be a professional at it to? How does she do that?
    o Do you have a chapter with frequently asked questions?
    o Do you have a 'before' chapter? What was life like before your innovation?

o Can you add a chapter about another case history?
o Do you have a miscellaneous tips chapter?
o Can you do a chapter where you analyze famous people?
o What are the current trends in your subject matter?

GETTING CUTER

There's not much to say about putting your chapters in order, but there are a few things worth saying about giving them titles that are more appealing.

If you need help coming up with chapter titles more attractive than something straightforward like "Looking for Holes In Your Business Plan", go back to the M-N-O-P-Q-R-S Test.

For the sake of your editor, though, use hyphenated titles. Put the cute title first, followed by a hyphen and the straightforward title. Here's an example:

"Kryptonite and Achilles' Heels—Looking for Holes in Your Business Plan"

CHAPTER SUMMARIES

The next section of a proposal is a summary of what each chapter will be about.

These chapter summaries build more evidence that you have enough material to fill a book. They also show off your writing skill. Use your most compelling material:

- If your book isn't written yet, use the future tense. "This chapter *will* examine the relationship between job satisfaction and overall health."
- In most cases, it's best to talk to the reader directly, referring to her as "you".
- Think in terms of benefits. How will the reader's life improve when he learns the lessons from this chapter?
- Impress agents and editors with how passionate you are about your topic.
- Show off how organized your thinking is.
- When possible, start each summary with one of the hooks on page 88.
- Show as many facets of your writing as you can. Be informative and entertaining, or be moving.
- Include words that appeal to the three main senses: seeing, hearing and feeling. Use phrases like "you'll see", "listen to" and "here's how to get your hands around this concept".
- Focus on the main point of the chapter and to write a few short sentences about the rest of the chapter.
- If you've got a great anecdote that makes a particular chapter's point, for God's sake use it, even if it takes you past the one page mark for the chapter.

SAMPLE CHAPTERS

The literature on writing book proposals offers widely varying opinions on which sample chapters to include. One book says to always include your first chapter. Another book says to never use it.

What's a poor, starving writer to believe?

My opinion is this: Think like a movie producer who is making a preview of his film. Which two chapters will make readers hungry to read your book? Which chave your most appealing or compelling anecdotes or case studies? Which are likely to have readers nodding their heads in recognition? Or laughing and crying at the same time?

These are the chapters to submit.

If you still can't decide, pick the chapters that are the easiest to write.

With autobiographies, choose chapters that create two different emotional moods.

If you decide to submit partial chapters, make sure they are obviously labeled as such.

Start each chapter with a hook. This is one of the signs of a professional writer.

If possible, end each chapter in a way that leaves the reader dying to know what comes next.

To do this, summarize what the reader learned in this chapter and give a brief description of the next chapter. For example, end a chapter with a sentence like this: "Now that you can charm women into wanting to get to know you better, it's time to find out how to have them yearning to talk to you without saying a single word."

Here are some writing mistakes to avoid:

1) **Don't use the same word to begin a sentence twice in a row.** After I wrote this last section, I found three sentences in a row that started with the word "if". I changed two of them. Vary your sentence structure.

2) **Don't say "I think" or "I believe".** It's your book. The whole thing is something that you think or believe. Instead of writing, "*I think people should be friends* for a few months before they get involved romantically", say "People should be friends" etc.

3) **Get rid of most or all of your "You shoulds" and "you needs".** Your reader already knows you are talking about him. Instead of "You should go to bed early", simply use "Go to bed early".

THE APPENDIX

Here's where you put the supporting evidence that proves you're a credible expert and a media darling.

You can include:

✓ Press clippings
✓ Highlights of reviews
✓ Endorsements of other books
✓ Testimonials from clients

- ✓ Testimonials from talk show hosts
- ✓ Mention any cassettes or videos you are submitting with your proposal, such as tapes of your talk show appearances or one of your keynote speeches.

CHAPTER 20

GETTING YOUR ACT TOGETHER
AND TAKING IT ON THE ROAD

Congratulations. You are almost ready to submit your book proposal to agents and editors.

You have three tasks left:

1) Hire a book coach to help you make your proposal the best it can be.
2) If you plan on being published by a large publisher, make a list of agents you want to submit your proposal to. If you have a book geared to a smaller audience, make a list of small publishers.
3) Write what is known as query letter to get an agent to request your book proposal.

First off, hire a book coach or an editorial service.

No matter how good a writer you are, you can't be objective about work you just finished.

Hiring a pro to look at your proposal could increase the size of your advance.

All five of the authors I know personally who received advances of $100,000 or more worked with professional book coaches or editors.

If you want to hire a book coach, you can find detailed information in Chapter 11. It offers less expensive alternatives, too.

You can also call me for coaching at:

The Authors Team.

(831) 458-1550

GetPublished@AuthorsTeam.com

http://www.AuthorsTeam.com.

PICKING AN AGENT

If you plan on getting published the traditional way, (by a royalty publisher who pays for the rights to your book) and you want a chance for a decent-sized advance, you need an agent. Here are three reasons agents are worth the 15% that they charge:

Agents know books. If an agent is representing your book, an editor knows that the material is worth looking at. Editors will read proposals from agents much faster than they will read submissions from unagented authors. You will get feedback faster and, ultimately, you will get published faster too.

Agents know editors personally. They may know something about an editor that could make the difference in selling your book.

For example, if you've written a book about keeping your self-esteem after your divorce, you might have an easier time selling it to an editor who has recently been divorced. You wouldn't know that about an editor, but your agent would.

Agents have leverage. They represent books by other authors, sometimes very big authors. The editor wants to publish these other books. She knows that if you don't get a good deal, the agent might not think favorably of her when she bids on a book from other clients of his.

She may offer him as much as 30% more for your book than she would offer you.

ONE REASON NOT TO GO WITH AN AGENT

If you have a book that serves more of a niche audience, you need to seek a smaller publisher. If these publishers offer any advance, it'll be small. Since agents make the bulk of their money from book advances, they don't work with publishers of this size. You'll need to represent yourself.

Two books you can use to find these publishers are the annual edition of *Writer's Market*, edited by Brogan and Brewer, and *Writer's Guide to Book Editors, Publishers, and Literary Agents, 2003-2004: Who They Are! What They Want! and How to Win Them Over* by Jeff Herman.

If you go this route, you still need a query letter. Follow all the suggestions below for finding an agent and sending query letters. (Where it says "agent", just substitute "publisher".)

FINDING AN AGENT

Here's the best way to find an agent suited to books on your topic:

1) Find books that are like yours.
2) Look in the acknowledgements section of each book to find out who the author's agent is. Make a note.
3) Look the agent up on the Web. If he doesn't have a website, look him up in Jeff Herman's book or *Writer's Market*. (See above.)
4) Make a list of the agents you want to query and their contact information.

Another useful resource is Publisher's Lunch, a free newsletter available at http://www.publisherslunch.com. This newsletter lists all the latest deals including the names of the agents who made them.

HOW TO GET REFERRED TO AN AGENT

If you want to have an edge when it comes to getting a literary agent, your best bet is to get referred to the agent by someone he knows.

Agent James Levine says that his agency reads all of their unsolicited manuscripts, but accepts only about one percent for representation. "Most of our clients are referred by other clients or by editors."

The best way to get referred to an agent is to hang around or correspond with authors. (This is also a good trick if you want to get endorsements to include in your book proposal.)

How do you do that?

1) Attend meetings of your local National Speakers Association chapter. Many speakers write books to enhance their speaking careers. If you start to hang out with these folks, you will be sneezing distance from dozens of authors. The national organization is at: http://www.nsaspeaker.org.

2) You can meet established writers at writers' conferences. Agents often show at these events, too. You can find a comprehensive list of conferences at: http://www.awpwriter.org/wcc/w.htm

3) Want to spend ten minutes with a publishing professional? You can do this for $40 at the Maui Writers Conference. http://tinyurl.com/601m

4) The Learning Annex often has classes about writing a book proposal. These are usually with agents, editors, or authors. This is a good way to make a connection. http://www.thelearningannex.com

5) Good book coaches have relationships with agents. They will be happy to refer you once your book meets their standards.

6) There are many authors you can start a correspondence with via their web site. Publishers often have links to these authors' sites. You can also do a search under the author's name to find an author's home page.

Keep your correspondence with authors about their book at first, until they get to know who you are. Then you can ask them if they would be willing to look at your two-page overview. If they like your overview, they may offer to introduce you to their agent on their own. If they don't offer, gently ask if you can wangle an introduction to their agent.

Query Letters

The letter you send to an agent to get him to request your book proposal is a query letter.

It needs to be a real attention grabber. Agents sometimes read these one hundred at a time.

All the material you need for a query letter is in the overview of your proposal. If your overview is more than a page and a half, shorten it to that size. Add a paragraph asking the agent to request your proposal. That will give you a good first draft of a query letter.

Here's the basic format:

1) Start off by saying "I am seeking representation   for _____." Fill in the title of your book along with a two sentence version of your book's hook.

2) Follow that with the reason you are querying this particular agent. Steps 1 and 2 form your first paragraph.

3) In the next paragraph, expand the description of your book and explain who will want to read your book and why.

4) Take a few sentences to say why your book is different from all other books on the subject.

5) Next, mention any promised endorsements or foreword.

6) Follow that by explaining why you are qualified to write this book.

7) If you have a sizable audience that knows you through your work with the media, internet mailing list, or ongoing speaking appearances, communicate that. (This is called your platform.) If you give seminars and can guarantee that you will sell a certain number of books as part of the cost of your seminars, mention that.

8) Do you have a marketing idea that is unusual? If you truly believe that it will make a difference in whether or not an agent is interested in representing you, put it in your query letter.

9) Finally, tell the agent how to request the proposal from you. If you want to create some urgency, use the exclusivity close from the query below.

Here is the letter Peggy Vincent sent to agents:

Dear _____,

I am seeking representation for a 400-page memoir, ***Baby Catcher***, an eye-opening, poignant, often hilarious romp through my fifteen years as a certified nurse midwife in Berkeley, California. (1-2 sentences about why I have chosen this particular agent)

The story begins with Zelda, a pregnant black woman in "Mr. Duke's hospital" in 1962 (excerpt attached). Similar in organization and anecdotal style of writing to James Herriot's memoirs, each chapter in ***Baby Catcher*** can stand alone. Taken from my experiences in delivering over two thousand babies, the stories are arranged like a crazy quilt of births in all their marvelous, often dramatic and sometimes frightening individuality. I sew the pieces together with the thread of my belief that women's bodies know more about having babies than their brains do. Given freedom and support, laboring women will find their own best way to give birth. I've laughed and danced with women and listened to them sing Golden Oldies through their labors. I've watched them clap their hands, bang on the walls, and backpedal crab-wise into a closet moments before giving birth. I've delivered the baby of a redheaded Scot in a thunderstorm on a leaky sailboat and cupped the bum of a breech baby in my palm in the back seat of a speeding car. But nothing in my conservative upbringing in the Midwest prepared me for midwifing a tattooed and multi-pierced centerfold model for an S&M magazine.

In spite of midwifery being known as 'the second oldest profession for women,' very few books by or about midwives exist. The huge success of Gay Courter's *The Midwife*, and Chris Bohjalian's novel, *Midwives*, chosen as an Oprah book, demonstrates that there is a wide audience for stories about midwives. ***Baby Catcher*** will fill the neglected niche of non-fiction writing on the subject. The two midwifery memoirs that are still in print and selling well are *Diary of a Midwife* by Juliana Van Olphen-Fehr and *A Midwife's Story* by Penny Armstrong. In a class by itself is the 'Amazing Birthing Tales' section of *Spiritual Midwifery* by Ina May Gaskin. For twenty-five years women have loved reading those birth stories, but many were turned off by the hippie language and counter-cultural lifestyle that the book espoused. *Baby Catcher*, written by a licensed midwife with one foot on the home birth side of the ideological fence but with the other one firmly planted in Western medical tradition, will have an even broader appeal.

Essayist Philip Lopate read three chapters of *Baby Catcher*, described them as 'superb and engaging,' and has agreed to provide a quote for the book jacket when it is published. Adair Lara, columnist for the *San Francisco Chronicle*, and Cathy Luchetti, author of *Medicine Women*, have also promised endorsements.

I will show this proposal (including three representative chapters) to only one agent at a time, so if you are interested in seeing it, please contact me right away by phone, pager, fax, or email. An SASE is enclosed for your convenience in replying.

Yours truly,
Peggy Vincent

AGENT ROULETTE

Now it's time to submit your query letter and your proposal to agents.

1) **If you have been referred to an agent by an author who is represented by him**, ask that author if you should send a query letter by itself or a query letter with your book proposal.
   If that author has gone to the trouble of contacting an agent to introduce you, submit material to that agent alone. Mention that you are submitting your material to him exclusively.
2) **Follow-up:** Call the agent's office after four weeks and *politely* ask for an update on your status. After six weeks of no response, send a letter to the agent explaining that if you don't hear from him in a week, you will be giving another agent the exclusive right to represent you.
3) **If you are sending query letters without a referral to an agent**, pick the top ten agents on your list and send a personalized query letter to each. (This is a modified version of Susan Page's system.)

When you hear from an agent, thank him, and mention that a few agents have called. Tell him that it will take a few days for you to decide who to send the proposal to first.

When two weeks are up, send the proposal and a cover letter to the agent you like best. Make sure you write the words "REQUESTED MATERIAL ENCLOSED" on the outside of the envelope.

Write a short cover letter that includes your hook, a reminder to the agent that he requested the material, and a few words again about why you picked this agent. Then use the instructions on how to follow up in step 1.

If none of the agents in your first round respond to your query letter, run it by a book coach (or a second book coach). Make the necessary changes and send it out to the next ten agents on your list.

FINAL CHECKLIST

Here are a few quick things to remember when you send your proposal out to agents:

1) Make sure your proposal is double-spaced. There should only be about 250 words per page.
2) Use a header for each of the pages of your proposal that states your book's title and your name.
3) Make sure your pages are numbered.
4) Don't staple or bind your pages together in any way. Use one of those big paper clips if you want. Agents and editors prefer loose copies of your proposal.
5) Enclose a self-addressed stamped envelope with the correct postage so the agent can send your proposal back.

READY, SET, GO

One last comment: As you will see from the samples included with this book, there are a variety of ways to put together a book proposal. You can even add some things that haven't been mentioned here. But if you alter the format, make sure you include all the ingredients mentioned. They are all essential.

YOU REALLY CAN LAND A BOOK CONTRACT FROM JUST TWENTY PAGES.

Please let me know how you do in your quest to get published. Comments and suggestions are also welcome. You can e-mail me at:
GetPublished@AuthorsTeam.com

SECTION III
SAMPLE BOOK PROPOSALS

A BRIEF INTRODUCTION

I am extremely grateful to each of the writers who have shared these book proposals, all of which sold to publishers.

You may recognize sections that I have quoted earlier in this book. I am repeating them because there is something powerful about reading all the parts of a proposal together.

I am unable to include the sample chapters that accompany these proposals, because the various publishers of these books own those rights, not the authors. Buy the books to see the chapters.

Some of the proposals are incomplete. Certain authors have asked me to remove portions of their proposals for a various reasons. I will explain before each proposal.

BABY CATCHER

Baby Catcher is an example of autobiographical material written by a complete unknown who hadn't given speeches, seminars, or appeared on television or radio. Nonetheless, Scribners bought it for over $100,000. It was submitted to eight publishers, four were interested and three actually made bids.

A complete unknown can actually sell a book to a large publisher for a six-figure advance.

Peggy Vincent, the author, took writing classes for two years before she started her book. She also hired a book coach to work with her on her proposal.

It certainly paid off!

BABY CATCHER
A BOOK PROPOSAL BY PEGGY VINCENT

OVERVIEW

What is *__Baby Catcher__* about?

The first time I saw a baby born, it was more magical to me than seeing a white dove fly free from the hands of a sorcerer – more magical because it wasn't magic. It was real. Since that day in 1962, I have nourished myself by tapping into the passion of women giving birth.

__Baby Catcher__, a 350-page narrative nonfiction story, cavorts with drama, joy, hilarity, and tenderness through my career as a certified nurse midwife. I 'caught,' as we midwives say, over 2,500 babies around Berkeley, California. As *__Baby Catcher__* progresses through nearly a quarter century of time, each chapter introduces a memorable woman who is busy negotiating her own unique path through childbirth. There's redheaded Megan giving birth on a leaky sailboat, creating a sense of instant home and family where previously there was just the smell of old fish. And Susannah, who delivers as easily as a chicken lays an egg. Meet courageous Erica, who begs the doctors to operate on her without anesthesia; speedy Polly, whose baby is born right after her panicked husband crams her into a VW bug; and prim Julie, who pronounces that the pain of childbirth is "interesting" as she affirms her religious beliefs by giving birth at home without drugs.

Whether a profound epiphany, a lighthearted tweak on some universal theme, a dramatic crisis resolution, or a simple, heartwarming tale of birth trivia, all of the stories share the feeling of the world moving aside to make room for one more soul. No other book captures so vividly the marvelous diversity of ways that individual women experience this otherwise similar event known as birth.

In spite of midwifery's reputation as 'the second oldest profession,' very few books by or about midwives exist, but the bestseller status of Chris Bohjalian's novel, Midwives, and the continuing reissue of Spiritual Midwifery 25 years after initial publication indicate an ongoing fascination with the subject. Pregnant women, mothers, and everyone looking for richly unusual stories will find their heartstrings resonating with the world depicted in *__Baby Catcher.__*

Suzanne Arms, filmmaker, international childbirth advocate, and author of the pivotal Immaculate Deception, will write the foreword. The following authors, all of whom have read material, have agreed to provide endorsements:

- Philip Lopate, author and essayist for The New Yorker
- Anne Lamott, author of the bestsellers Bird by Bird and Traveling Mercies
- Marshall Klaus, international speaker and author of Maternal-Infant Bonding
- Adair Lara, author and columnist for the San Francisco Chronicle
- Cathy Luchetti, author of Medicine Women.

In addition, Chris Bohjalian, best-selling author of Oprah-pick <u>Midwives</u>, has agreed to read the manuscript of ***Baby Catcher*** in January, 2001, with the intention of offering to write jacket copy.

My years of hospital experience prior to the takeover of obstetrics by high-tech machines, as well as my 15 years attending home births, allow me to straddle the dichotomy that exists between the medical model of birth with its focus on the science of childbirth, and the midwifery model, which pays equal heed to the artistry of birth. In ***Baby Catcher***, as well as in my midwifery practice, I find it easy to balance the conflicts that often separate these ideologies.

Baby Catcher, however, is more than a memoir. The book chronicles the childbirth movement from the time when white men controlled obstetrics and dragged babies like limp mops from the bodies of drugged women, through the Lamaze and natural childbirth eras, into the years when alternative birth centers popped up like dandelions – and finally to the decade when we midwives had the best of all worlds. We had hospital privileges, physician backup, and malpractice insurance that covered us for both home and hospital births. That era is now history, and ***Baby Catcher*** is my celebratory offering to the women (and men and babies, and nurses and doctors) who made those years so special.

Organized into eight thematic divisions, ***Baby Catcher*** follows a linear structure as I evolve from naïve student nurse to self-confident, independent midwife, learning at each stage that the women themselves are my best teachers. The first two segments of ***Baby Catcher*** telescope the years from my introduction to obstetrics in nursing school in 1962, to my graduation from midwifery school in 1980. Readers meet unforgettable Zelda, a wise-beyond-her-years, backwoods black woman who kindles my awareness of women's struggles to gain control of their own bodies; and oh-so-proper Mrs. Purdue, my nursing instructor who gets down and funky with the best of 'em as she curses her way through a precipitous delivery. These early chapters relate my discovery of rampant pedophilia in a tarpaper shack in North Carolina and the very different births of my first two children, one complicated and violent, the other painless. Part Two concludes as I unexpectedly deliver my friend Maria's baby on the toilet, because the regular midwife arrives too late.

The remainder of ***Baby Catcher*** transports the reader into a fascinating world that only a very small number of people ever experience – the world of a midwife doing both home and hospital births in a unique urban area, rushing from the hospital delivery of a teenage welfare mom, to a dot com millionaire's mansion overlooking the Golden Gate Bridge. Among many unusual characters, there is Hallie, a tattooed astrologer married to a paraplegic; Teri, a butch-dyke lesbian who rises to fairy godmother status; and a hyper grampa who nearly burns the house down as he cooks breakfast for eight.

The home birth of my third child comes near the middle of the book and is followed by a desperate cross-town trip in my nightgown two days later to catch a baby who has hopped onto the fast track. A heartbreaking stillbirth concludes this section.

At the peak of my career, a Good Samaritan act results in a lawsuit that threatens my career, as well as that of all midwives doing home births in the United States. From the pivotal chapters describing that tragic birth, ***Baby Catcher*** winds through the last three years of my private practice. Readers meet Elizabeth and Guido, a pair of ex-heroin addicts who choose to have a baby as an affirmation of their new life, and Rosebud and Vinnie, the 400-pound black prostitute and her skinny, cross-dressing partner who struts through the prenatal clinic showing off his flashy earrings and tight, leopard print pants.

In the epilogue, a brief discussion of the current status of midwifery in the U.S. segues into one final birth, that of a devout, young Muslim woman. As her intention to become a midwife in the Middle East coincides with the end of my midwifery practice, I give her my obstetrical textbooks, figuratively passing the torch to the next generation of baby catchers.

Baby Catcher concludes with three appendices. The first, Pearls of Wisdom, offers an amusing but revealing collection of midwifery one-liners, the kind of tips that veteran midwives pass on to their apprentices, such as: redheads bleed, slow starters are often fast finishers, and – my own personal favorite – it's far better to be lucky than smart. The second appendix is a list of the supplies I carried in the four boxes that made up my midwifery kit. Appendix III is a straightforward resource list of relevant organizations, books, and videos.

Readers who pick up ***Baby Catcher*** will feel like invisible observers, staring wide-eyed through a keyhole into a wonderful world that is usually open to only a privileged few. The book offers an amazing journey of revelation to the casual reader as well as to the more obvious audience of pregnant women, mothers, and obstetrical professionals. Men, too, report being captivated. After I read the chapter 'Cut Me!' to a large group of writers, one male statistician, a bachelor, commented, "When you started to read your story, I thought, 'Oh, no, another vagina story!' but it wasn't like that at all! I loved every word."

A first draft of the entire manuscript of ***Baby Catcher*** has been completed. The final revision will be ready within six months of receipt of the advance.

Author
Who is Peggy Vincent?

As a new writer, I found homes quickly for my articles in:

The Christian Science Monitor
Mothering Magazine
The San Francisco Chronicle
IParenting.com

Prior to seeking publication, I took nonfiction writing classes at UC Berkeley, as well as a series of classes for 'master writers' from Adair Lara, columnist for the San Francisco Chronicle. In October of 1999, I attended a conference in Santa Fe where Philip Lopate led my seminar. At the end of the workshop, he offered to write jacket copy for ***Baby Catcher***. In February, 2000, I attended the Southern California Writer's Conference in San Diego where I three chapters from ***Baby Catcher*** and received **first prize for nonfiction**.

* * * * *

After catching over 2,500 babies – babies of all colors and sizes, babies born in locations varying from a sailboat to a migrant shack, babies born to fundamentalist

Christians, lesbians, Muslims, and indigent welfare recipients, as well as stay-at home moms and professionals struggling to balance commuting to Silicon Valley with raising kids – I retired from midwifery in 1995, with gratitude for the many gifts that I had received. These gifts include seeing girls turn into women as they come to the end of their first labor, helping dads deliver their children into their own hands, and sharing the wide-eyed innocence of a toddler sitting in her granny's lap – the gift of being present at one of life's grand, transitional moments, time after time after time.

It all started in the obstetrical department of Duke Hospital in 1962, and by the time I graduated from nursing school two years later, I was hooked on the passion and drama of birth. Marriage followed, and then a move across the country to Southern California. After working for four years as a public health nurse in the Hispanic barrio of East Los Angeles, my husband and I lived abroad for a year. When we returned to the States during the hippie era, we scampered out of LA and zipped up the coast to the San Francisco Bay Area, where we've lived ever since.

Alta Bates Hospital in Berkeley became my professional home for the next 20 years, first as a staff nurse and charge nurse in the delivery room, and then as the **director of the first alternative birth center in the East Bay**. During those heady years of the birth center movement in the Bay Area, I realized that a midwifery career was the inevitable next step. So I went back to school, graduating in December 1980, from the University of California's certificate program of nurse midwifery at San Francisco General Hospital.

Upon graduation, my feminist and entrepreneurial spirit led me to open a solo home birth practice, utilizing a supportive physician at Alta Bates as back up for emergencies. In 1984, I became **the first midwife in the East Bay to succeed in obtaining hospital delivery privileges**, and for the next six years, I offered both home births and hospital births to my patients.

In 1991, following a crisis within the malpractice insurance industry, I sadly closed my private practice and took a position as staff midwife at Kaiser Hospital in Walnut Creek, California. However, I continued to attend several home births each month, until my retirement in 1995.

I believe a good measure of my success and acceptance by the conservative medical community stemmed from my traditional training and my years of hospital experience. Most home birth midwives start out as lay midwives before becoming nurses and then licensed midwives; many of them never spend any significant time working within a hospital. Hospitals exist as a world unto themselves with their own codes of behavior, language, and hierarchy. I grew up with those codes and felt comfortable in settings that midwives from alternative backgrounds often found intimidating.

During my long years of interacting with the childbearing population, I taught hundreds of natural childbirth classes and gave lectures to groups both large and small on a wide range of topics, encompassing everything from birth control to breastfeeding.

I live in Oakland with Roger, my husband of 35 years, and our home-born, teenage son, Skylar. My older son, Colin, and my daughter, Jill, her husband, and their daughters live nearby.

AUDIENCE

Who will buy *Baby Catcher?*

Women never tire of telling their birth stories and are hungry to hear the stories of others. *Baby Catcher* targets women. All women. But particularly women in their childbearing years, as well as those millions of mothers who still remember the precious moments surrounding the births of their children. But as birth is a universal theme, an adventure that crosses all cultures, social classes, religions, and races, the reading audience clearly broadens far afield from the topic of childbirth and midwifery. *Baby Catcher* is a plain old 'good read.' There's something for everybody - drama, humor, excitement, stories that bring on tears and laughter – even for those who have never had any baby experience.

Women who may be considering hiring a midwife for their next birth will read *Baby Catcher* to learn about the broad scope of midwifery practice as well as the intimate details of touch, laughter, and caring that make a midwife-managed birth so wonderfully different. Those women who have already experienced the kind of special delivery that only a midwife can offer will find stories within *Baby Catcher* that make them rejoice once again for the choices that they made. In 1998, licensed midwives delivered 10 percent of all babies born in this country. Lay midwives account for an additional few percentage points.

Six percent of childbearing women in the United States planned a home birth in 1998. Women considering this option will read *Baby Catcher* either as a validation of a choice they have already made or as an additional resource in their decision-making process.

A large part of the population currently uses some form of alternative medicine. That same population is likely to be interested in midwifery, which has never been viewed as part of mainstream medicine in this country. *Baby Catcher* will further their knowledge of midwifery as a viable health care option. Likewise, many chapters of *Baby Catcher* will appeal to individuals interested in feminist topics and women's health issues.

Midwifery is a labor of love, and midwives never tire of talking about their jobs. There are 7,000 licensed midwives in the United States and over 1,000 lay midwives. Within the pages of *Baby Catcher*, each of them will find confirmation of her belief system, as well as a joyful celebration of the art of midwifery that midwives alone can appreciate. The hundreds of thousands of obstetrical nurses in this country will also discover many of the stories ringing true to their own experiences.

Baby Catcher crosses all socioeconomic, ethnic, and religious lines. The language in the book is neither condescending nor loaded with medical terminology and can therefore be enjoyed by medical and lay people alike. As *Baby Catcher* doesn't display a strong bias on either side of the home birth/hospital birth controversy, obstetrical professionals of all persuasions will discover something within these pages to make them smile and feel proud of their calling to serve women and babies.

COMPETITION

What books will compete with ***Baby Catcher***?

Very few books by or about midwives exist in the current market, and those that do have become backlist items. ***Baby Catcher***, written by a licensed midwife attending both home and hospital births in an urban area, will fill a large gap in the market, especially since the few books about midwifery that are in print have a much more limited focus or appeal.

Revolutionary when first published in 1975, Spiritual Midwifery by Ina May Gaskin remains in print, having gone through many reissues and several new editions. However, the book's hippie language, its rural communal farm setting, and the midwives' pride in their lack of formal training now make the book seem dated.

Two other first-person books written by midwives that grace the shelves of bookstores have both received five-star reviews at Amazon. A Midwife's Story by Penny Armstrong remains in print 12 years after its 1988 publication. An engaging tale of a traditionally trained midwife attending home births among the Amish communities of Lancaster County, Pennsylvania, the book limits its focus to this small, rural, religious sect. Most modern readers will find it easier to identify with the diverse population of the San Francisco Bay Area in ***Baby Catcher***.

Juliana Van Olphen-Fehr's linear memoir, Diary of a Midwife, published in 1998, records the political skirmishes and major battles that she fought along the road to her midwifery career. Ms. Van Olphen-Fehr's book lacks the strong human dimension of ***Baby Catcher***, which avoids a political tone and focuses on the intimate, compelling, and dramatic birth stories themselves.

There are two novels whose strong sales and sustained popularity point to an interest in midwifery by the reading public. Chris Bohjalian's Midwives, featuring a lay midwife in rural Vermont, jumped onto the bestseller list when it was chosen as an Oprah recommendation. And Gay Courter's The Midwife, a work of fiction based on a Russian Jewish immigrant at the turn of the century, is still in print more than a decade after publication. While neither should be construed as competition to a contemporary nonfiction book such as ***Baby Catcher***, their continuing availability demonstrates an unfulfilled appetite for the subject matter of midwives and childbirth. Written by a licensed midwife with one foot on the home birth side of the ideological fence but with the other one firmly planted in Western medical tradition, ***Baby Catcher*** will feed this appetite.

MARKETING

How will ***Baby Catcher*** reach the public?

Many possibilities exist for publicizing ***Baby Catcher*** to a specialized audience as well as to a general trade readership. Ready-made outlets exist for publicizing ***Baby Catcher*** in the many organizations and institutions specializing in obstetrical care, alternative medicine, women's health issues, and feminist topics.

The convention of the American College of Nurse Midwives meets yearly, and the book sale tables always generate brisk interest. I will attend in order to assist sales of ***Baby Catcher***. Their 20-page quarterly newsletter, Quickening, will be an ideal spot for an in-depth review. Similarly, NACOG, the nursing division of the American College of ObGyn, meets annually, and I will plan to attend.

There are two main natural childbirth organizations in the United States, ASPO (American Society for Psychoprophylaxis in Obstetrics) and AAHCC (American Academy of Husband-Coached Childbirth). They are more commonly known, respectively, as the Lamaze and the Bradley methods. Both organizations have newsletters and hold regional meetings and national conventions. The newsletters are always looking for copy and will provide an ideal outlet for articles and excerpts from ***Baby Catcher***. Book sales receive much attention at the annual conventions of both organizations, and I will attend in order to promote ***Baby Catcher***. Additionally, the 5000 teachers reach untold millions of women yearly through their frequent and well-attended birth classes. Reading lists are included in the handouts for these groups, and I will endeavor to insure that ***Baby Catcher*** appears on these lists.

There are more than 40 regional and national midwifery newsletters, some targeted to licensed midwives and others focusing on lay midwives. All of them look for news to fill their columns. I will write an article about ***Baby Catcher*** and make certain that it is available to each one of these newsletters.

Copies of ***Baby Catcher*** can be excerpted and reviewed in nursing and midwifery magazines, such as American Journal of Nurse-Midwifery, Nursing Outlook, American Journal of Nursing and the Journal of Obstetrical, Gynecological and Neonatal Nursing. Their combined readership exceeds half a million.

Trade magazines such as Parenting, Family Circle, Women's Day, McCalls, and Ladies Home Journal, read by over 50 million women each month, will also provide an excellent outlet for reviews and excerpts from ***Baby Catcher***.

The quarterly alumni letter of Duke University lists publications authored by graduates, and I will make certain ***Baby Catcher*** receives prominent mention. Additionally, Duke Magazine, published six times a year, reaches 80,000 alumni annually. Both publications will be interested in reviewing this book, written by a graduate of the university.

I look forward to advertising in RTIR (Radio-TV Interview Report) and receiving invitations to speak on talk shows in the local and national media. I am eager to assist in the promotion of ***Baby Catcher*** and will travel and attend as many readings, book signings, public appearances, and interviews as I can.

RECOGNIZING EXCELLENCE

Recognizing Excellence was published as *Make Their Day: Employee Recognition That Works* by Berrett-Koehler, a smaller press that specializes in books about management and human resources.

Cindy Ventrice tells a bit about the story of how she got published in chapter 1.

The section Cindy titles "Knowledge Base" is worth noting. It shows Cindy's research and gives her additional credibility as an expert.

Cindy doesn't want the general public to see her gentle critique of competing books, so only the overview of how her book differs from others on the topic is included.

RECOGNIZING EXCELLENCE
HOW TO INCREASE MORALE, PRODUCTIVITY AND PROFITABILITY USING EMPLOYEE RECOGNITION
A BOOK PROPOSAL BY CINDY VENTRICE

Subject:

Most employee recognition is a dismal failure that leaves peak performers feeling inadequately recognized. Organizations set up costly and ineffective recognition programs that try to buy employee loyalty and performance. Individual managers make erroneous assumptions about what employees want. When recognition efforts fail, managers say that recognition doesn't work.

This book will demonstrate that high impact recognition requires committed leaders, managers and supervisors, rather than complex systems. Through extensive interviews, the author will provide numerous examples of how effective recognition requires leaders dedicated to making recognition a priority, and managers and supervisors who will take the time to build excellent working relationships with their employees.

Need:

Last year, most organizations were focused on retaining employees - - all employees. Turnover rates varied from 10% to 150% annually depending on the industry. Salaries went up, job satisfaction went down, and turnover rates remained high. Money didn't solve the job satisfaction problem. Employers were desperate to increase job satisfaction in order to keep employees.

Today, in an effort to be more profitable, organizations are laying off workers, reducing incentive pay, and trying to accomplish more with fewer people. The frustration and uncertainty that employees are experiencing have further eroded job satisfaction. Employee morale is at an all-time low and the emotional and financial costs of low morale are negatively affecting productivity and profitability.

Employers are searching for ways to keep morale high while staying profitable. Employee recognition is an important part of the solution to this dilemma. Done well, recognition cultivates job satisfaction, improves morale and commitment, and leads to a more productive workplace.

Leaders, managers, supervisors, and small business owners need a quick-reading, nuts and bolts book that demonstrates the difference between high impact recognition and the recognition programs that have failed them in the past.

Administrators need a guide to help them work with managers to create and administer effective recognition on an organization-wide basis.

Purpose:

    1) To provide managers, supervisors, and small business owners with the information that they need in order to offer high-impact recognition.

2) To provide administrators with a tool that will help them administer successful organization-wide recognition.

3) To provide trainers with a resource appropriate for supervisors and managers on the topic of employee recognition.

These three purposes will be achieved by presenting materials that:

- Challenge existing thought about effective recognition.
- Explain what really motivates employees and what organizational factors may be undermining recognition efforts.
- Demonstrate which key elements must be in place in order for recognition to be successful.
- Help the reader assess the current state of recognition in their organization and/or department.
- Guide the reader through the development of high impact recognition.
- Provide ideas for recognizing employees.

Most recognition fails or receives lukewarm enthusiasm because managers and program administrators don't understand what motivates employees. This book is designed to overcome the obstacles to *successful* recognition.

New Contribution:
While many books offer recognition ideas and describe the mechanics of a recognition program, no other book has focused on the failure of organizations to ensure that employees feel adequately recognized. This book looks at what's missing and shows how to integrate recognition into the organizational culture using leadership and relationship management.

This book will offer:

- A description of why recognition frequently fails.
- Information on the role of leaders, managers, administrators, and individuals in recognizing high-performance.
- Proven examples of what works and what doesn't.
- Ideas that range from free to high-ticket/high-impact awards.
- Tools and case studies for improving recognition.

According to the Center for Creative Leadership, less than 50% of managers *ever* give any form of employee recognition. Many managers think recognition doesn't work, and in many organizations it doesn't. This book will help organizations turn ineffective recognition into high-impact recognition.

Competitive Publications:
There are no publications that complete directly with the proposed book. There are many books that focus on rewards without delving into the underlying issues of recognition.

No publication:

- Emphasizes the importance of individualizing recognition for each employee.
- Examines the role of every individual in creating high-impact recognition.
- Focuses on the role of relationship in recognition.

Audiences and Uses:

For leaders, managers and supervisors interested in improving employee morale and increasing performance, for administrators in charge of overseeing a recognition program, and as a resource for seminar participants.

Primary audience - mid-level managers to entry-level supervisors 18,170,000 in U.S.

Secondary audiences - administrators and trainers responsible for employee recognition

Associations -

ASTD (my article on this topic will be in their 2001 yearbook) 55,000 members

SHRM - 63,000 members

EAC – (I have spoken to EAC audiences of 50 – 200 people at various Northern California EACs) Every employer in California receives EAC mailings from the EDD.

IPMA (has offered to review finished book) 6,500 members

ODN - 3,700 members

AWBA American Small Business Women's Association - 70,000 members

NAWBO National Association for Women Business Owners - 6,000 members

ASBA American Small Businesses Association - 150,000 members

Knowledge Base:

As a long-time consultant and trainer, the author has had the opportunity to work closely with hundreds of companies, government agencies and non-profit organizations in both advisory and project management positions. She has experienced first hand both the need and impact of recognition in motivating employees, particularly when the organization is undergoing change.

The author has worked with:

Employees that consider themselves burned out, offering training and coaching on self-motivation.

Workshops –

Coping with Burnout.

Preventing Burnout.

How to Reignite Passion in the Face of Frustration.

Managers and supervisors, offering training,consulting and coaching on employee motivation.

Workshops -

Improving Job Satisfaction with Rewards and Recognition.

Five Strategies for Attracting and Retaining Peak Performers.

Managing Employee Expectations
Improving Morale during Times of Change

Association leaders, offering the presentations and workshops –
Inspiring Volunteers.
The Leadership Survival Kit.

Interviews:
Employees - The author has interviewed numerous employees regarding the impact of recognition that they have received. These high-impact anecdotal stories will be used to highlight key points in the book.

Managers - I am in the process of interviewing managers from various organizations distinguished for their recognition programs.

Interviews to date:
> **Microsoft Great Plains Business Solutions** - listed as one of Fortune's 100 Best Companies to Work For 2000. Fargo, ND
> **Graniterock** - listed as one of Fortune's 100 Best Companies, for the past four years. Winner of the Malcolm Baldrige Award 1992. Watsonville, CA
> **Viking Freight** - a subsidiary of FedEx known for high levels of employee satisfaction. San Jose, CA

Some planned interviews:
> Container Store –Dallas, TX
> Xilinx – San Jose, CA
> Vanguard Group – Valley Forge, PA
> Whole Foods Market – Austin, TX
> SAS Institute – Cary, NC

I have studied the problem of low employee morale, as well as the latest research into what creates a satisfying work environment.
> Some of my resources include:
> ***Books:***
> First, Break All the Rules - Marcus Buckingham & Curt Coffman
> Commitment in the Workplace - John P. Meyer & Natalie J. Allen
> Intrinsic Motivation at Work - Kenneth W. Thomas
> Contented Cows Give Better Milk - Bill Catlette & Richard Hadden
> Love 'Em or Lose 'Em - Beverly Kaye and Sharon Jordan-Evans
> The Truth About Burnout - Christina Maslach & Michael P. Leiter
> Managing Transitions - William Bridges
> Getting Around Bureaucracy - Lorraine Monroe
> Rewards That Drive High Performance - Thomas B. Wilson
> 301 Ways to Have Fun at Work - Dave Hemsath & Leslie Yerkes
> Abolishing Performance Appraisals – Tom Coens and Mary Jenkins
> ***Articles:***
> Seven Deadly Demotivators - Dean Spitzer, Management Review 11/95

Tech Worker Wish List - Washington Post 12/1/99
A Company Where Workers Have a Life - Mercury News 1/21/01
Winning the War to Keep Top Talent - Fortune 5/29/00
Re-energize the Disengaged Worker - InfoWorld 4/16/01
100 Best Companies To Work For - Fortune 1/8/01
Miscellaneous:
Diverse resources with examples of recognition as a motivator include Fast
Company and Toastmasters magazines.
Dilbert cartoons - always a source of inspiration on how *not* to motivate
employees.
Malcolm Baldrige award criteria
Drake Beam Morin survey 1/21/01
McKinsey & Co. War for Talent 2000 - survey
Emerging Workforce 1999 study

The author has written several articles on recognition and employee morale. They
appear at www.potential-unltd.com. Some published articles are included with the
proposal. The author is a contributor in ASTD's Training and Development
Yearbook, McGraw-Hill, to be released October 2001.

Biography

Cindy Ventrice, President of Potential Unlimited Seminars, has been providing
consulting and training services since 1984. Her work has brought her into close
contact with organizations of nearly every size and industry, including technology,
nonprofit, government, health care, service, and tourism. She assisted these
organizations as a consultant, project manager, team leader, and trainer.

Her work as a consultant and trainer provide Cindy with invaluable insights into
communicating a vision, motivating employees, bringing diverse personalities and
skills together to create an effective team, and managing effectively from a distance.

Cindy is active in the training community. She is currently serving her second
year on the board of ASTD-Silicon Valley and will serve as President-Elect for 2002.

In addition to consulting and training, she is a frequent public speaker and a
member of the National Speakers Association.

Cindy is a contributor on the topic of Individualizing Recognition in ASTD's
Training & Development Yearbook, October 2001, McGraw Hill.

She lives in Santa Cruz, California.

Introduction - Bev Kaye and Sharon Jordan Evans (or another from endorsement
list)

PART ONE – EMPLOYEES WANT TO LOVE THEIR WORK
Chapter One - Money doesn't buy loyalty or performance
Pay as an incentive - the solution that didn't work
Defining the motivation problem
How job satisfaction impacts performance

Why employees really leave (it's rarely about money)
Intrinsic vs. extrinsic motivation
Does this mean money doesn't matter?
Awards and plaques aren't the answer
Why most recognition leaves employees dissatisfied
Recognition scorecard - How well are we doing?
Recognition isn't a band-aid
"If I praise them they'll want more money."
Other excuses for failing to recognize employees

Chapter Two – Recognition is inherent in the work
Recognizing purpose
Recognizing quality
99% of *Immunex* employees are proud to say where they work
Recognizing trustworthiness
Flexible scheduling at *American Management Systems*
Recognizing team work
Team members at *Whole Foods*
Recognizing potential
Working at *Cisco Systems*
Organizational danger signs
A motivating work environment is a form of recognition

Chapter Three - Recognition is about relationships
Everything else is secondary
Why *The Container Store* was Fortune's #1 Best Company of 2000
Employees have their say about recognition
Recognition from HR is meaningless
We can tell when the boss doesn't mean it
The most meaningful form of recognition
How does your organization measure up?
How to interpret lack of employee enthusiasm
The danger of inter-company competition
Sincere recognition breeds loyalty
Xilinx employees take out a full-page ad

PART TWO – RECOGNITION – WHOSE JOB IS IT ANYWAY?
Chapter Four – Leaders provide vision and momentum
Create a recognition culture
Southwest Airlines' recognition culture
Lead organization-wide recognition
How it's done at *SAS Institute*
Show support for recognition efforts

Chapter Five - Managers and supervisors have the power to recognize
Responsibility for success or failure belongs to the manager

Managers at *CDW Computer Centers* go out of their way to recognize staff
Recognition doesn't require organizational support
Laying the foundation – the manager/employee relationship
Managers at *Synovus Financial* care about employees

Chapter Six - Human resources... the best department in a supporting role
Why recognition should never originate with Human Resources
Supporting organizational recognition
Survey, analyze and track
How *Fedex* administers recognition
Doomed before you start - recognition without management's support
Safeguards can improve success

Chapter Seven - Recognition is the responsibility of every employee
Catching the recognition bug
Peer recognition
Informal
Nominations
The *Microsoft/Great Plains* story
Employee designed recognition
Charles Schwab
A case study in responsibility for recognition

Chapter Eight - Self-recognition - an innovative concept
A look at how *Graniterock* approaches recognition
Recognition Days
The Independent Professional Development Program
Asking for recognition

PART THREE - RECOGNITION THAT WORKS
Chapter Nine - A lesson from a fortune cookie
Make recognition specific and relevant
What do values have to do with recognition?
The Microsoft Great Plains Heritage Award
Values help avoid unintended results
Employees want to be both *valued* and *valuable*
Communicating values at Raytek
Tie recognition to performance
Shared goals and performance
Individual goals and performance
High-performance behaviors
Measure for results
What to measure
What are you currently measuring?
What others are measuring

Data collection
    Review of financial and operational documents
    Questionnaires and surveys
    One on one interviews
    Focus groups
    Observation
Specific recognition

Chapter Ten – One-size-*doesn't*-fit-all

Personalized individual recognition
    People want to do work that matters
    People want their unique abilities and interests recognized
    Everyone benefits
Individualizing recognition - a three step process
    Step 1: Identify how the individual can contribute
    Step 2: Determine what the individual values
        Interviewing for preference
        After the interview
        Interview everyone
    Step 3: Recognize their unique contribution with personalized rewards
        How would you like to be rewarded?
Case study - when recognition misses the mark.
    What went wrong?
    What could Terrence do differently?
    Ideas for rewards

Chapter Eleven – Putting a price tag on recognition

Big budget recognition
Low-cost recognition
No-cost recognition

Chapter Twelve – Recognition is a work in progress

Effective recognition requires planning and commitment
Start small, observe, evaluate, adapt
Planning for recognition
    Job satisfaction surveys
        Questions successful companies are asking
        Analyzing the results
    Establishing a recognition budget
    Setting realistic goals and timeframes
    Communicating criteria and rewards
    Tool - recognition checklist
Where do you go from here?

Appendix

Supporting documents
Recommended reading

Manuscript Length and Special Materials 150-180 pages with tools, examples, graphics, charts and illustrations.

Timetable: To be completed by July 31, 2002.

Author's marketing efforts:
As a speaker and trainer, I will self-market this book to my audiences, both through corporate paid engagements, and unpaid association engagements.

As a board member of ASTD-Silicon Valley, I will promote the book through ASTD channels available to me, including direct mail and speaking at conferences and workshops.

I will continue to publish related articles. Attached are articles that have been published to date.

Articles scheduled for publication:
- ARA Recognition Review, November 2001 – Individualizing Recognition, pt 1
- ARA Recognition Review, December 2001 – Individualizing Recognition, pt 2

I am currently working with the following publications on fitting articles into their editorial calendars for 2002:
- ARA Recognition Review – Paying Attention to the "Soft Stuff."
- Vitality Magazine (free to employees in many corporations) – Coping with Burnout, Managing for Retention, and Improving Morale with Recognition and Reward.
- Manage Magazine – Managing Employee Expectations.
- Office Solutions - Paying Attention to the "Soft Stuff," Managing Employee Expectations, Conflict in the Workplace, and Employee Recognition.

Other marketing efforts:
- Appropriate radio and TV interviews
- My website (www.potential-unltd.com)
- My on-line newsletter recipients
- Book talks and signings

Endorsements:
The author will solicit supportive quotes about the book from two or more thought leaders such as: (Cindy included a list of about twenty people who are known nationally or very specifically in her field.)

EXTREME SUCCESS

Rich Fettke met with *Extreme Success* when he submitted this proposal to publishers. Eight asked him for meetings. We'll never know how many of them would have made offers for this book, because Simon and Shuster did what is called a "pre-empt". They made an outstanding offer contingent on Rich accepting it without looking at any others.

One way you can tell that Fireside (a division of Simon and Shuster) was really behind this book is the beautiful cover. The design is top-notch; but the tell-tale sign is the lettering. Rich's cover may be the only one I've ever seen with embossed metallic letters.

The first thing you'll notice about Rich's proposal is the power of endorsements. Rich has a lot of them and his proposal starts off with one from bestselling author Cheryl Richardson.

The other thing you will notice about this proposal is the writing. It is extremely engaging. Rich doesn't take the easy way out anywhere. Even the marketing material has the tone of well-written advertising.

The parts that are missing are the sections on Media and Publicity, the Competition, and Promotional Ideas. Rich is working on a follow-up that uses some of those ideas, so he doesn't want to give away any proprietary information.

Even so, you get a darned good idea why Simon and Shuster was willing to part with over a hundred grand to land this book

EXTREME SUCCESS

A BOOK PROPOSAL BY RICH FETTKE

ENDORSEMENTS FOR *EXTREME SUCCESS*

"Rich Fettke is a publisher's dream—bright, good looking, nationally known, and a talented speaker and writer. His book, ***Extreme Success***, fills an important gap in the self-help business—the practical steps needed to build powerful partnerships that help us reach our goals with greater joy and ease! As a matter of fact, during the past year, more than 75% of the reporters I've interviewed with (over 500 of them!) have requested more information on how to create effective and supportive partnerships for success. Rich Fettke and his new book answer that question head on!"
—Cheryl Richardson, author of the #1 *New York Times* bestseller *Take Time for Your Life*

"***Extreme Success*** and Rich Fettke's approach is paramount for our times. This is the faster and easier approach for getting what you want."
—Marcia Wieder, author of *Making Your Dreams Come True*

"Rich Fettke is a pioneer in the coaching profession. Being an extreme thinker when it comes to life, Rich is one of those souls who 'lives out loud.' He models in his world what he writes about in this book. A must read for those who want to break free!"
—DJ Mitsch, President, International Coach Federation

"Rich Fettke's ability to inspire and lead is nothing short of uncanny, and his gift for helping folks conquer their fears is unsurpassed. Rich's creativity, warmth, integrity, and true grit afford him the opportunity to share some unusual gifts. Though it's clear he has fire in his belly, there's a rare kind of strength in his soul. His book shows us how to find this strength—and work with others—to easily reach our most cherished goals."
—Michael Gerrish, author of *When Working Out Isn't Working Out*

"***Extreme Success*** is the book for the new economy. With extreme sports as the new phenomena for Gen-Xers, now there is a way to approach success in the same way . . . and Rich Fettke is the man to lead folks in this new world. As a leader in the coaching industry, Rich has been on the cutting edge— extreme in his own way. You'll love this book, and you'll especially love him."
—Jennifer White, author of *Work Less, Make More*

"At last! A book with specific ways for people to enjoy the process of accomplishing their goals. Whether your desire is to improve your income or your life, Rich's ideas are sure to make the path a lot easier. As one of America's top coaches, Rich knows what it takes for people to create extreme success…without struggling."

—Lee Glickstein, author of *Be Heard Now!*

"Rich Fettke's message is very timely, as the rapid growth of the coaching profession proves. People need to learn how to be better partners in the dance of life and business. Their ability to achieve with ease improves through the power of partnership and Rich's message is such. It is one the public needs to hear."
—Laura Berman Fortgang, author of *Take Yourself to the Top: The Secrets of America's #1 Career Coach*

"With all the books on self-actualization, I'm delighted to see a book that also shows how our relationships are vital to realizing success in business and in life. Rich is the perfect person to bring these ideas into the marketplace. In addition to being a dynamic speaker and masterful coach, I can personally attest to his ability to be a leader that inspires both growth and action in individuals and groups."
—Marcia Reynolds, past president, International Coach Federation, author of *Capture the Rapture*

"Rich Fettke is an inspiring speaker and a leader in the field of personal coaching. Consider yourself lucky to have him as your 'Extreme Success' Coach!"
—Talane Miedaner, author of *Coach Yourself to Success*

"Rich Fettke brings a passion and dedication to the realms of learning, coaching and partnership that are so important to the development of human effectiveness this decade. Rich is most creative and holds a rare and futuristic perspective on the potential of personal success."
—Laura Whitworth, author of *Co-Active Coaching*

OVERVIEW

I was ready to push my limits, to succeed at something I had never done before. That meant boarding the waiting airplane and pushing myself through a cargo door while cruising at 90 mph at 14,000 feet.

I stood at this brink for one reason: I wanted to break through the unfounded terror I had about doing a solo skydive out of an airplane. It wasn't as if I hadn't tried other boundary-breaking excursions. After all, I had bungee-jumped off the Golden Gate Bridge and rock climbed sheer cliffs. But this was different. I really wanted to push my limits, based on what I knew I could do—but the idea threw bolts of stark terror inside me.

As I stood there, struggling with my fear, my skydiving instructor walked over. "Hi, I'm Billy," he drawled, offering his hand. About forty, with a three-day growth of beard, he wore a T-shirt that said SKYDIVERS: Good to the Last Drop.

My stomach sank along with the image of myself plummeting towards my inevitable meeting with very hard ground. Undaunted by my no doubt terrified expression, Billy went over the safety instructions carefully. Finally, we put on our parachutes, boarded the plane and up we went. The higher we climbed, the faster my heartbeat.

"Remember," Billy yelled at me over the howling wind, "if you ever start to panic or struggle just stop, be aware and resume control." Nodding, I took a deep breath and then shouted out the protocol: "Ready…set…go!" Billy and I jumped out of the plane into one of the most life-changing events of my life.

Billy held onto me until we reached 6,000 feet. Then he let go so that we would have enough room to open our parachutes. As soon as I was on my own I heard that familiar nagging voice of fear that tortured me. "What are you doing out here alone?" the voice taunted me. "You're going to screw up—and that means you're going to die."

All of a sudden my body flipped and I started to tumble over and over as I frantically grabbed for the ripcord. But the harder I tried the more I missed it—and the closer I fell to the quickly approaching ground.

Then I remembered Billy's words. Stop. Be aware. Resume control.

In that moment I stopped struggling. I corrected my position, found the ripcord and pulled it. Phoomph! A huge multi-colored canopy mushroomed above me as I floated gently to earth.

I yelled in triumph as I touched down. Not only had I overcome my fear-- I had done it twice. Once, before I jumped and once after. I achieved what I came to refer to as **extreme success,** that is, redirecting my strengths and dramatically expanding my success into new areas. At the same time, I overcame the nearly overpowering sense of struggle that almost prevented me from fulfilling my goal.

I learned an invaluable lesson that day. I discovered that struggle doesn't make success happen. In fact, struggle can prevent success from happening.

This is the basis of the philosophy I've adapted for my life—and the heart of my business. I've learned how to redirect strengths and neutralize struggle so that achieving greater success is possible. Like me, my clients have learned how to do this. And now, so can you.

EXTREME SUCCESS:
THE NEW GOAL FOR HIGH-ACHIEVERS

As a personal coach I guide ambitious men and women toward reaching ever-higher goals. Through the process of deeply getting to know my client's values, goals, dreams, and personalities, I've observed several characteristics that prompted me to define them as "Extreme Achievers." They are people with an intense desire to achieve high profile success and get the most out of life. My observations and research into this group led me to some fascinating findings.

☐ Extreme Achievers are usually between the ages of 25 and 40. This means a majority of them are from Generation X—America's 44 million people between the ages of 25 and 36. As the MTV generation, they crave fast, fun and simple information. <u>As a member of this group, I understand what drives them as well as how to communicate with them.</u>

☐ Extreme Achievers are often 'adrenaline junkies." Thrill-seeking sports junkies who invented bungee jumping, they brought boundary-breaking outdoor sports like rock climbing, skydiving, mountain biking, snowboarding and extreme skiing into the mainstream. <u>As a risk taker, I understand how adventure-filled sports stories and metaphors will appeal to this group.</u>

☐ Extreme Achievers believe that pragmatism rules. The most important piece of information is "will it work?" Real-life answers to their real-life questions are what they seek. <u>That's why I provide practical and proven solutions in an easy-to-absorb format.</u>

☐ Extreme Achievers organize their lives and then organize some more. Palm Pilots, pagers, cell phones, date books blocked out for six months or more—these are the accessories of choice because schedules and timetables rule. Not surprisingly, a widespread side effect of hyper-organization is mega-stress. <u>To combat this all-too-common syndrome, I present new ways to focus on what really matters.</u>

☐ Extreme Achievers yearn for fulfilling relationships. Since many are the offspring of divorced and/or busy working parents, they value the ideal of meaningful partnerships. Simultaneously, many lack the skills to make those happen, much less work. <u>I show how to develop relationships that provide the support they need to accomplish their most important goals with greater ease.</u>

. ☐ Extreme Achievers crave real stories of people like themselves. Identification with others sharing their feelings gives them an enormous sense of belonging and direction. <u>My book is filled with first-person stories of the challenges and breakthroughs of my clients—and myself.</u>

There is one other common element that the Extreme Achievers I work with share: they believe that attaining goals requires long, hard hours of devotion and concentration, often at the expense of their personal lives. Part of my job is to convince them otherwise. To do that, I give them the simple tools they need to build on what they have. Consequently, they achieve high profile success without struggle and keep it without burning out.

Using true client stories, I'll show how my Extreme Success system works, as it did for:

☐ Tamara, the owner of a large gymnastics school and rock-climbing gym. Despite her success, Tamara was plowing all her money back into her businesses and spending most of her time with them, to the exclusion of her family and personal time. Facing these dilemmas with an Extreme Success strategy, she was able to cut down her presence at work while her ventures grew. The time she spent with her family increased, as did the opportunities to participate in the sports she loved. Best of all, she took herself away from work—all the way to Nepal—for a vacation.

☐ Michael, a partner in a television commercial production company. With $30,000 of credit card debt he wanted to pay off, Michael needed help. Implementing Extreme Success lessons, he made the important shift from working in his business to working on his business. In only eighteen months he raised his company's income from $50,000 to over $1 million a year.

☐ Christine, a financial advisor at a Fortune 100 investment firm. After eight years in her profession, Christine was feeling burned out. Her income had stabilized and she felt like she had no time for herself. She said that "life was lukewarm" and that she wanted to "live again." Using several Extreme Success habits, Christine broke free from boredom and burnout. She lost over twenty pounds, met a wonderful man, and at the same time increased the growth of her business by 200% over the previous three years combined.

Basically, Tamara, Michael and Christine learned one fundamental lesson: they learned how to stop struggling against themselves.

THE STRUGGLE SYNDROME

The belief that struggle is an inseparable partner of success is deeply ingrained; it's something I hear from just about all my clients. When I ask them why they feel this way, they usually say, "My parents always told me that if I wanted to make it big I had to work hard. And every time a colleague succeeds, you always hear someone say, 'Wow, he really worked hard for that. He deserves the recognition he's getting."

At the same time, I noticed how so many self-help books and seminars promote persistence, breaking through obstacles and yes, even struggling.

So it's not surprising that so many people assume that success has to be painful. Unfortunately, because of this assumption, they begin to create their own struggling strategies.

This doesn't mean that I don't believe in challenge; I do. There's nothing I embrace more than the thought of achieving something new that's going to require real effort. What I don't believe is that effort automatically links with struggle, which further links to negativity. All struggle produces is a situation where enjoyment is sucked out of what you're doing—even if the outcome is successful.

I know there's a much more effective and joyful way to live and work.

Identifying the Struggle Syndrome

You don't have to leap out of an airplane and lose control to feel the impact of struggle. My coaching clients report lots of various struggle syndrome symptoms. Headaches, a tight neck, snapping at co-workers, an untidy car, forgetting appointments, losing things—these are all signs.

I know when my own struggle bug starts to bite. I clench my jaw, jump from project to project, and stack file upon file on my desk. Not surprisingly, when this happens I become distracted while feeling overwhelmed and even frantic. Now, however, when the symptoms first kick in I'm aware of them and I stop them quickly by saying a simple phrase to myself: "How can I make this easy?" This helps me to step back, become more aware, and begin to enjoy what I'm doing.

One of the most common manifestations of the syndrome is that distressing "voice" – I call it the "Protector" – that starts talking the second you have doubts. Maybe you believe that the voice is your eternal enemy—when you don't believe it's actually your ally and doing you a favor.

Actually, you're right on both counts. The Protector has always been on the job and it has a long memory. Ever vigilant, it records every failure and disappointment. Its job is to prevent disaster from happening to you again. Unfortunately, it doesn't realize that the humiliation you experienced in 7th grade gym class has nothing to do with your presentation in front of a group of venture capitalists. So, whenever that voice starts broadcasting over your mental airways, acknowledge its protective role and then answer it. Tell it that the goal is something you want and you'd like the Protector to help you. Ask it how you can succeed without it trying to hold you back.

Remember: the Protector is part of you, so use it as your partner.

THE POWER OF PARTNERSHIP

Besides viewing the Protector as a partner, it's imperative to join with others in order to succeed. I'm going to show you the most effective ways of partnering that will give you:

☐ Accountability, which helps us take the action we know, deep down, is best for us.

☐ Structure, which provides the discipline to follow through on that action.

☐ Support, which keeps us going until the goal is accomplished.

☐ Leverage, which helps us do more than we can on our own.

☐ Knowledge, which moves us faster and more easily toward our goals.

Ultimately, identifying the struggle syndrome, taming the voice within, and linking with partners will tap into the formula for achieving extreme success. By doing so, you'll learn to rebalance yourself.

REBALANCING THE STRENGTHS YOU HAVE: THE KEY TO EXTREME SUCCESS

I don't believe that we have to suffer from our "weaknesses." I've learned from my own challenging business and personal experiences that unlimited success is just a matter of redirecting the strengths we already have in other directions. That means taking what I call a "wide-angle" view of yourself, and approaching goals with the knowledge that you already possess what you need to succeed. Most of all, it means being true to who you are.

My Extreme Success System

My life has been, and continues to be, filled with "extreme" activities that challenge me. Ocean jet skiing, competitive bodybuilding, power lifting, and wakeboarding are some of the sports that build on what I've already accomplished. But tackling on-the-edge sports is just one risk area of my life. When I was twenty-three I opened a large health club near Boston, sold it at a profit when I was thirty and moved to California to begin a new life as a personal coach and professional speaker.

Through all the ups—and downs—of my life, I've identified five basic factors that lead to the path of extreme success. They are:

☐ There are no limiting weaknesses, only lack of the right attitude and focus. By learning how to turn perceived "weaknesses" into strengths, pushing limits without struggle can become easy. I'll show you how it's done.

☐ Opportunities can be created. The key is redirecting past successes and strengths into new areas. That way, when opportunities arise, all the preparation will have been done. I'll reveal the path where preparedness intersects with opportunity and take you to the place where you can create your own "luck."

☐ Taking risks is just as important as preparation when it comes to expanding success. This is where my Calculated Risk Index comes into play. I'll help you clarify what to do, when to do it, and how to avoid the pitfall of over-preparation.

☐ There's no such thing as a self-made success. Everyone needs partners for support and creative give-and-take. There are effective ways to use partnerships and alliances; I'll show you what they are and how to form them.

☐ Focusing your attention on your intention is the path to success. Unfortunately, many people let their attention be drawn away by struggle in lots of different ways. Encompassing everything from disorganized offices to listening to the "I should" mental list, struggle wastes a lot of time and energy. I'll reveal how letting it go can reap huge rewards.

Filled with real-life stories, self-quizzes, and the 30-Day Extreme Success Challenge, which offers step-by-step strategies, *Extreme Success* is the blueprint for your unlimited future.

FORMAT

Extreme Success will provide inspiring, practical and proven solutions in a fast, fun and easy-to-absorb format. With illustrated sidebars featuring key statements, boxes and cartoons, the reader can get the ideas they want without struggle.

The book will have seven sections with about twenty chapters on how to push your limits and reach your highest goals without struggling. Each chapter will contain real-life stories of challenges and breakthroughs of my clients and myself, along with captivating extreme sports stories and metaphors. I envision the book as a 5.5" x 8.5" hardcover of approximately 200 pages.

ABOUT THE AUTHOR

A media-genic business expert who has been featured in numerous magazines and newspapers including *USA Today*, *the Wall Street Journal*, *Self* and *Entrepreneur Magazine* and has also been a guest on every major TV network and on dozens of radio shows including *NPR*, *SPN* and the *Dr. Laura Show*, **Rich Fettke** helps people push their limits and expand their success without struggle. Over the past five years thousands of people have participated in the workshops and seminars of this record-holding extreme sports athlete.

One of the country's top success coaches, his diverse clientele includes IBM, Chevron, Prudential, Century 21, and the United States Army. Rich's speaking programs include "The Power of Coaching," "Getting and Staying Focused" and "The Courage for Change."

His keynote seminar, "Extreme Success," is also offered as a ten-week goal achievement program. At the initial four-hour workshop, participants use rock climbing or rope courses as metaphors for learning how to create supportive partnerships, overcome fears, take action, stay focused and achieve greater success both personally and professionally. Afterwards, participants meet in weekly group meetings on a special telephone bridge line to discuss their goals, get live coaching and to support each other in achieving their most important objectives.

Rich is past-president of the Professional & Personal Coaches Association and was one of the first twenty-five coaches to receive the Master Certified Coach credential from the International Coach Federation. He has over fifteen years experience in business start-ups, management and training and holds a bachelor's degree in Business Administration with a specialty in Business Management from Merrimack College in Andover, Massachusetts. He is also a graduate and former instructor of The Coaches Training Institute, the world's largest, non-profit and accredited coach training organization.

As a member of the National Speakers Association and the International Federation of Professional Speakers, Rich travels nationally to present his ideas to corporations and associations.

He is author and narrator of the audiotape program, *FOCUS: A Guide to Clarity and Achievement* and has written numerous articles on personal and professional success.

Rich lives near San Francisco with his wife and two daughters and Zen, their dog.

THE MARKET

The strongest target group for *Extreme Success* is made up of young business people with strong entrepreneurial spirit and an intense desire to achieve high profile success at work. At the same time, they seek fulfilling personal lives. Hungry for "success secrets," they search for valuable information in books, at programs and seminars and on the Internet. As industry mavericks that drive change, extreme achievers often run their own companies or work for an aggressive corporation where they are responsible for their own business development. They aim to scale the corporate ladder as quickly as possible before jumping over to another company for higher pay, more generous benefits and greater recognition.

Constantly searching for ways to improve their effectiveness and speed up their success, extreme achievers often struggle to become successful on their own. A faster, easier, more supportive solution is what they seek. This makes the market for *Extreme Success* wide and deep, encompassing:

☐ **Self-employed people,** whose numbers continue to grow, having almost doubled since 1980 to over 17 million. One of the biggest challenges of the self-employed is the lack of structure and accountability to follow through on important tasks. Many complain that they feel like they are "all alone" in their business lives. *Extreme Success* gives self-employed people ways to develop the support they need and proven strategies to stay focused and effective on their most important goals.

☐ **Business partners,** who currently make up over 1.6 million non-incorporated business partnerships in the United States. Highly competitive dot-com companies and business startups are forming every day. More and more people are realizing that they can leverage their assets by partnering with others. *Extreme Success* offers business partners strategies to improve communication, use individual strengths more effectively, achieve goals and get more from collaborative efforts.

☐ **Young executives,** who are experiencing the fast-paced, constantly changing new business climate of the 21st century. The old way to achieve success was to make a plan and then work that plan. That scenario doesn't play anymore; there are too many variables in the marketplace. Opportunities are being created every moment out of thin air. *Extreme Success* teaches young executives how to break free from limiting perspectives of the past so they can be prepared to act on the best opportunities in their future.

☐ **Sales people,** who must develop the courage and motivation to network, make phone calls and give presentations. The Bureau of Labor Statistics estimates a total sales force of over 13 million nationally. Some experts estimate that as many as 100,000 new salespeople enter the labor force each year. Salespeople are constantly searching for new ideas and strategies to help them stay motivated, break through fears and build their sales. *Personal Selling Power's* readers' survey shows that salespeople purchase a median of six books per year primarily in the area of success motivation. *Extreme Success* offers inspiring ideas for salespeople to improve their motivation and shares proven tools that they can use to immediately better their results.

One of the most powerful tools that *Extreme Success* gives sales people is a way to create a success partnership with someone else in their (or another) industry.

☐ **Business, personal and executive coaches,** who number over 30,000, continually search for new skills and ways to work with their clients. This group collectively reaches millions of business people every year. As a highly visible leader in the field of coaching, my innovative techniques and ideas are sought after by my peers and shared with their clients. As a result, hundreds of coaches will purchase *Extreme Success* and recommend it to their clients, which will result in exponential sales growth.

CHAPTER SUMMARIES

INTRODUCTION

Because extreme success and extreme sports are linked like a parachute to a ripcord, I'll show how adventure stories make apt metaphors for achieving what you want in business and life. In extreme sports, you can decide to have the process be a struggle or a joy – before you even put your hand on a cliff or tie a bungee cord around your ankles. The same principle applies in work and life.

How you can get the most out of this book is up to you. I suggest that you read the whole book and take the self-quizzes to better grasp the extreme success concept. Some of what you read may go against the conventional "success lessons" of the past. Remember: in many ways, things are different than they used to be. To cope with, and take advantage of, our ever-changing world, we must find new strategies for success.

So, after you read the book I suggest you go back and "work" it. Create "action items" based on what is most important to you. Finally, take on the 30-day Extreme Success Challenge. This will help you shift strategies from ideas to action and from action to results.

PART ONE
X Marks the Spot: The Path to Extreme Success

1) Extreme Success and Luck: The Link You've Been Waiting For (chapter included)
2) Breaking Out of the Struggle Syndrome
3) Balancing Extremes to Expand Your Success

This section introduces a new perspective on how to achieve greater success without long, hard hours of devotion and concentration. It also explains how to experience more joy while progressing faster toward reaching important goals. It's about changing the mindset that achieving success means that you must struggle to reach your goals and dreams. I'll give you the match to lighting the fire of success without burning yourself out in the process.

Also, I'll explain how limits are created by the struggle we fabricate in our minds. We often generate this struggle so that we don't have to take the risk of doing what needs to happen to create the success we desire. And, because I believe that being in the right place at the right time is not an accident, I introduce the "X" model for accomplishing extreme success. One line of the X represents preparation; the other represents opportunities. The intersection of the two is the place where calculated risk, action and courage are required. When all of these areas come together we create what some people call "luck." Once this intersection is reached, you are ready to move into the zone of extreme success—without struggle.

This section also explains what it means to balance extremes. Most people have areas in their lives where things are going very well and other areas where things are lousy. For example: a great relationship but a terrible financial situation, a high level of fitness but a low level of education, an incredible income but no time to share with the kids. Balancing extremes means creating incredible success in *all* areas of your life as opposed to a single area of focus. I'll show you how to do it.

Part Two
Get Ready to Go Big: Preparing Yourself for Opportunities
4) Redirecting Your Strengths to Conquer Your Weaknesses
5) Developing the Courage for Change
6) Bringing Out the Best of Who You Really Are

Before you begin to move toward creating deliberate luck and extreme success, it is necessary to strengthen and prepare yourself physically, mentally, emotionally and spiritually, the same as you would when preparing to participate in an extreme sport.

Here are strategies for self-support, how to develop your character and personal strengths and redirect those strengths to overcome your current self-imposed limits. Forget about those "minuses" you may think you have. You can redirect the plusses to bolster any less-than-perfect areas. It's essential to face goals with the knowledge that you already possess the instruments of success. I'll show you how to be prepared to notice opportunities when they present themselves and be ready to take the necessary action.

Part Three
Don't Do It Alone! Teaming Up for Success Without Struggle
7) An Easier Way (chapter included)
8) The Power of Partnerships
9) The Advantage of Alliances

In rock climbing, it's imperative to have a partner to point out moves you may not see, to challenge you to take action and to hold your rope in case you fall.

Partnerships also go hand-in-hand with extreme success. A success partner can provide support, help clarify objectives, prompt action and encourage you to overcome struggle. With this support, you can maintain focus on your goals.

In this section I'll tell you how to choose a quality success partner, how to form and maintain the partnership and what tools and structures can help you make the most of the relationship.

I'll also explain how to form alliances with people who will share their experience, knowledge and contacts to help you move toward your goals with more speed and ease. I'll show you step-by-step strategies on how to overcome any resistance or fears of approaching someone to create an alliance. Pointers on what to say, what not to say and what to do after an alliance is formed are included.

Part Four
Look Where You're Going: Seeing Opportunities Through a Wide Focus
10) Hocus Focus: The Curse of Over-Planning
11) Standing at the Edge: Putting Attention on Your Intention

When you are getting ready to crank down a trail on a mountain bike at full speed the first step is to clarify where you plan to complete your ride and to look for any hazards, such as trees, fences and big drop-offs, as you ride. In the same way, getting clear on what you want to work toward, and how you want to develop, are significant elements of extreme success.

This section helps develop the skill of wide focus, that is, seeing the big picture so that opportunities don't pass by and future hazards don't plunge you into the struggle syndrome. I'll outline ways to look into the future to determine what today's next steps should be without getting stuck in the limiting view of over-planning. Having a compelling vision of what you want in the future, and getting clear on what needs to happen right now, is a vital step in creating the joy of being in the present moment. The result is more ease, because you will know you are closer to the future you envision.

PART FIVE

Remember, Fear is a Four Letter Word: Turning Resistance Into Action

12) Enter the "Protector"
13) Using F.E.A.R. to Your Advantage
14) Jumping Off the Bridge (or stepping over the line)

Once you know how to prepare yourself, develop new strengths, increase awareness, build strong partnerships and clarify what you want, you are ready to face the "Protector." The self-limiting inner voice of impending doom, the "Protector" can hold you back from reaching your goals and dreams and trip you into the struggle syndrome. The most powerful tool the Protector uses is fear.

Common thinking says that you can beat this negative talker by not listening to it. This will not work. The way to deal with the Protector is to learn how to use it. This section will show you how to turn resistance and fear into a positive, energizing force for your success.

To do that, I'm going to give you a new definition of fear. The four key steps to overcoming the resistance and fear of change are:

Focus
Explore
Assess
Respond

Expanding success has less to do with preparation—which is still important—than with overcoming fear and raking risks. This is where my Calculated Risk Index (CRI) comes into play. An interactive self-quiz that helps you to see when you are being foolhardy and when you are being smart when it comes to risk taking, the CRI prevents you from getting stuck in indecision and aids you in making better choices based on your current reality. It clarifies what to do, when to do it and how to avoid the pitfall of over-preparation.

PART SIX
Stay in the Zone: Maintaining Focused Momentum
15) Avoiding the Accountability Addiction
16) Re-Zoning Takes Extreme Energy
17) Do Today What Brings Joy Tomorrow
18) Extreme Success, One Habit at a Time

One of the greatest "highs" of sports is that flow state often described as "being in the Zone." Those who have been there describe an almost mystical experience that results in, among other things, increased confidence, heightened awareness, total concentration, and near-effortless momentum. In the Zone, time seems to stand still and focus is unwavering.

This is a fundamental goal of high-achievers for good reason. If you are out of the zone, your mind has a tendency to drift from being focused, diverting attention to irrelevant or even negative thoughts.

This section shows you how to maintain focus and how to be in the Zone more often. You will learn how to keep your attention on what you truly want, why the common model of setting goals doesn't work, how to use targeted mantras to improve your focus and how to find a challenge-skill balance so you don't become overwhelmed, frustrated or ineffective.

PART SEVEN
What a High! Attracting On-Going Success
19) In a Moment, It Could Happen
20) The Higher You Climb the More You See

From the top of a mountain the view is spectacular. However, when you get to the summit, you can see many other peaks available for you to climb. This section discusses how the journey is actually the destination, and how to enjoy the process of facing new challenges with greater awareness and ease.

THE COURAGE TO LAUGH

This proposal is for Allan Klein's fourth book, which was published by J. P. Tarcher in September 1998. When you read it, you get the feeling that Allen has book proposals down to a science. Everything he does is right on the money.

Even in this brief proposal, Allan's life story comes across as moving. He is a man whose wife helped him keep laughing even though she was dying of cancer. He has gone on to help others keep laughing through difficult situations with his writing and teaching.

Allan mentions spin-offs in his book proposal. This is a wise idea. Agents and publishers are always on the lookout for a book that can become a series.

Klein also includes a section on reimbursable expenses. If you anticipate spending money that you want reimbursed, include a section like that.

THE COURAGE TO LAUGH
HUMOR, HOPE AND HEALING
IN THE FACE OF DEATH AND DYING
A BOOK PROPOSAL BY ALLEN KLEIN

Overview

The Courage to Laugh examines the lighter side of a not-so-funny subject. It provides inspirational anecdotes and unusual information about humor in the death, dying and the grieving process. It will give readers hope to rekindle their spirits and a sense of power over a powerless situation.

Bestselling authors such as Bernie Siegel, MD, author of Love, Medicine and Miracles, who has consented to provide a cover blurb for The Courage to Laugh, and Rabbi Earl Grollman, author of Living When a Loved One Has Died, have both touched upon the value of humor in serious illness and loss, but, until now, no book has dealt with the subject in depth.

The Hook

"Life," said George Bernard Shaw, "does not cease to be funny when someone dies, any more than it ceases to be serious when someone laughs." The Courage to Laugh expands on these words with spirited and funny examples from a world where many think there is no laughter. In the process, the book will prove that with humor, death and dying can be less of a grave matter.

Based on the health care seminars I have been presenting for the past ten years, The Courage to Laugh will be the first book to:

- show how patients and others use humor to cope when life is threatened.
- offer hope and encouragement to readers dealing with loss.
- give readers permission to laugh when they feel like crying.
- illustrate how popular culture can ease death-related fears.
- discuss how some cultures use humor to teach death and dying concern
- provide uplifting death-related quotes and jokes.

The Courage to Laugh will provide both humor and hope in a seemingly hopeless situation. When people are going through a life-threatening crisis they get stuck, like a Shakespearean drama, in the tragic fourth act. This book, like a Shakespearean comedy, is the redemptive fifth act. It will show readers that death is part of life and as such contains not only the tragic but the comic as well.

Length of Book

The finished manuscript will contain 220 pages divided into 12 chapters. There will also be 10 cartoons which the author will select and acquire permission to use.

The backmatter will include a bibliography, an index, and a page with my company's address and on-line number inviting readers to submit their stories, testimonials or suggestions for follow-up books.

Spin-Offs

A follow-up book called The Courage to Keep Laughing will contain new anecdotes submitted by readers and workshop participants. A series of books containing light-hearted stories related to specific illnesses (such as cancer, heart disease, Alzheimer's) is also a possible spin-off.

A companion audio tape album containing the uplifting stories in The Courage to Laugh. Ideally, these stories would be read by a variety of well-known actors and actresses.

Marketing and Promotion

Self-Promotion and Sales

- Authors Jack Canfield and Mark Victor Hansen (Chicken Soup for the Soul) have proven that a career as a professional speaker can greatly enhance the sales of the speaker's books. As a professional speaker myself, I have a multitude of opportunities to promote, publicize and sell The Courage to Laugh.

- As an award-winning speaker, I address over 7,000 people a year nationwide. Within the past year alone I have spoken in such major cities as Chicago, Houston, Knoxville, Los Angeles, Louisville, Mobile, New Orleans, New York, Portland, and San Francisco. My publisher and I can coordinate media interviews and book signings with all of my speaking engagements.

- I have a large following in the health care and the death and dying fields. In addition to speaking five times at the National Hospice Organization's annual convention, I have also spoken at state and local hospices in 22 states, hospitals in 37 states, and long term care conferences in 16 states. My current speaking engagements are likely to increase as my popularity continues to grow in the medical arena.

- I have developed a new speech based on The Courage to Laugh. I have already presented this talk several times and will continue to offer it to future clients, and expect that this speech will lead directly to back-of-the-room sales for this book.

- I will continue to maintain high visibility and sales for The Courage to Laugh over the next few years by giving keynotes presentations and workshops at both state and national conferences. I can arrange with the coordinators of these programs (at least 50 per year) for the book to be purchased for all attendees, or for it to be made available for back-of-the-room sales.

Media

- As a successful professional speaker, author and business owner since 1984, I am experienced in marketing my own products and services. Upon publication of The Courage to Laugh, I will publicize the book to the 3,500 meeting planners on my speaker's mailing list, to the 3,500 members of the

National Speakers Association (of which I am one of the highest ranking members) and to the thousands of members of the National Hospice Organization and the American Association of Therapeutic Humor.

- The juxtaposition of humor and death is a unique paradox that will attract media attention. I witnessed the immense appeal of this idea while on the publicity tour for my first book. Although The Healing Power of Humor devotes only a small section to death and dying, the chapters on humor and death repeatedly caught the interest of interviewers and frequently monopolized the conversation.

- I have been written about or quoted in such publications as *Ladies Home Journal, USA Today, New Age Journal, Woman's World, Bottom Line, Health Confidential,* and numerous newspapers, newsletters and magazines across the country. I have also appeared on CNBC-TV and over eighty regional radio and television talk shows nationwide.

- Following the publication of The Courage to Laugh, I will take out advertising in the Radio/TV Interviewer Report in order to generate nationwide media interest. An ad, which cost approximately $250, was placed for The Healing Power of Humor. It lead to several dozen radio show interviews nationwide.

- Beginning next month, I will be gaining national attention with the publication of Chicken Soup for the Grieving Soul (the next book in the "Chicken Soup" series). Four of my stories are featured in this book, including one that will appear in The Courage to Laugh.

Catalog Sales

The Courage to Laugh will be featured in *The Whole Mirth Catalog*-- a compendium of humor-related products which I publish, and which will be distributed to 15,000 people.

The Whole Mirth Catalog will buy a minimum of 1,000 copies of The Courage to Laugh in the first year of printing. It will continue to purchase at least 500 books a year for the following three years.

The Courage to Laugh would also be an ideal selection for several other catalogs such as HumorResources published by the Humor Project, and the book catalogs produced by both The National Hospice Organization and The Association of Death Education and Counseling.

Author's Track Record

Over 135,000 readers know my past books and therefore constitute a strong potential readership for The Courage to Laugh. My previous books include:

- The Healing Power of Humor (Tarcher/Putnam, 1989). A classic in its field. It is being used in classrooms and is recommended by the health care industry nationwide. It is now in its fifteenth printing (59,000 copies). In addition, foreign rights were sold to Spain, Denmark and Japan. The book was also a hardcover selection of the Rodale Press Book
- Club.Quotations to Cheer You Up When the World is Getting You Down. First published in quality paperback by Sterling Publishing Co., Inc., in

1991 (5,000 copies) and republished in a hard-cover edition by Random House Value Publishing in 1994. It is now in its fourth hard-cover printing (52,000 copies).

- Wing Tips. Recently published this year by Random House Value Publishing. 18,000 hardcover copies in the first printing.

Who Will Buy this Book?

In addition to the 135,000 people who have read my first book and my audiences of 7, 000 people each year, the following groups would also be the target market:

- The general public whose interest in the once-taboo topic of death and dying themes has already been established by past successes of such books as Elisabeth Kubler-Ross' On Death and Dying and, more recently, Sherwin Nuland's How We Die (The latter was on the *New York Times* bestseller list in both hardcover and paperback for 25 weeks.)
- The patients and staff in the 8,000 hospitals, 2,600 hospice programs and 16,000 nursing homes in this country. Patients will gain hope by reading The Courage to Laugh. The staff, who may already know that laughter helps them get through the day, will gain validation to continue seeking this powerful coping tool.
- Potential readers include the families and friends of the more than 340,000 patients who are served by hospice each year, the 48.9 million disabled Americans, the 9,360,000 survivors and those dealing with cancer, and the almost 500,000 people living and dying with HIV and AIDS.
- Hospital gift shops would be an ideal secondary market for those families and friends looking for a book to bring both humor and hope to the patients they visit.

Endorsements

Bernie Siegel, MD and author **Jack Canfield** have both agreed to provide a quote for the cover.

Others authors who know my work and would provide endorsements are:

      Stephen Levine (Who Dies?/Doubleday, Inc.)
      Carl Simonton, MD (Getting Well Again/Tarcher, Inc.)
      Vera Robinson, RN (Humor and the Health Professions/Slack, Inc.)
      Judy Tatelbaum, MSW (The Courage to Grieve/Lippincott & Crowell)

Competitive Books

At this time, there is a great deal of interest in books pertaining to humor and books dealing with death but little, if any, competition for The Courage to Laugh which examines both of these subjects.

Love, Medicine & Miracles by Bernie Siegel (Harper Perennial, revised 1990). This book explored how "exceptional cancer patients" take control of their situation. Humor is mentioned as one coping and healing tool but the main focus of this book is on other ways that cancer patients deal with their illness.

Chicken Soup for the Grieving Soul by Jack Canfield and Mark Victor Hansen (Health Communications, 1996). This soon to be published book contains heart-warming and inspirational stories concerning loss and grief. Some of these have a bittersweet quality which might evoke a smile or a laugh but again, as in the Siegel book, humor and loss are far from the main focus of the book.

Although there is not much competition for The Courage to Laugh, there is continuing interest in books about death and dying. The popular bestselling book How We Die by Sherwin Nuland (Random House, 1993) and the forthcoming publication of Start the Conversation: The Only Book You Will Ever Need about Death (Warner, 1996) are but two past and present examples.

My first book, The Healing Power of Humor, also briefly discussed the paradoxical subject of humor and death. But no book, until The Courage to Laugh, has explored the full therapeutic value of humor in loss. As shown by the figures in the marketing section, there is a large number of potential buyers who can benefit from this healing information.

Resources Needed to Complete the Book

A.   Time

The manuscript will be completed within eight months after signing.

B.   Expenses

Long distance phone calls to interview patients	500
Permission fees	1,000
Typing, manuscript assistance, research	2,500
Total	$ 4,000

About the Author
I am a professional award-winning speaker:
- In my ten year career as a professional speaker on the healing and coping benefits of humor, I have addressed nearly 100,000 people in 49 states across the country. My main clients are primarily in the health care field but I have also spoken to such well-known organizations as Motorola, Cornell University and the IRS.
- I am the recipient of two awards for my speaking expertise- a Toastmasters' International Community and Leadership Award (1985-86), and, a Certified Speaking Professional designation from the National Speakers Association (1993). Less than 8% of its 3,500 members hold this honor.
- In addition, in 1993 I was named Member of the Year of the northern California chapter of the National Speakers Association and served on its board of directors for two years.

I am a published author:

- In addition to my three books, <u>The Healing Power of Humor</u>, <u>Quotations to Cheer You Up</u>, and <u>Wing Tips</u>, my articles on the subject of death and humor have appeared in *Hospice Magazine, The American Journal of Hospice Care*, and *The Journal of Nursing Jocularity.* Other articles have appeared in *Prevention, Vegetarian Times, The Toastmaster, The American Druggist* and *The San Francisco Examiner/Chronicle.*
- Starting this Fall, I will have a regular column on humor and loss in *The Forum Newsletter* published by the Association of Death Education and Counseling.

Why I am the one to write this book:

The desire to write <u>The Courage to Laugh</u> emerged from a lesson I learned during my wife's terminal illness. Because of her keen sense of humor, she showed me that laughter can ease pain, lift us above our upsets, and soften our suffering. In other words, when we are in pain and wish that something would "take us away from it all," humor does exactly that.

This experience of losing a loved one, along with my former and current careers, plays a major role in this book and makes me the ideal person to write it. My expertise in the death and dying field comes from my positions as the Director of the Life/Death Transitions Institute in San Francisco, a licensed home health aide, and a hospice volunteer. My current professional speaking career provides me with a wealth of stories to enrich <u>The Courage to Laugh</u>.

Previous to the above careers, I was a scenic designer for CBS television. I designed such shows as Captain Kangaroo, Jackie Gleason and Merv Griffin.

I hold a Bachelor of Fine Arts degree from Hunter College, New York, and a Master of Human Development degree from St. Mary's College, Minnesota. I write and reside in a 110 year-old Victorian house in San Francisco.

I would like to write at least three other books based in part on my other popular seminars. Each book would take twelve to eighteen months to write, and would be completed in the order dictated by the publisher and market interest:

<u>Growing Down: What Kids Can Teach Adults</u>

Children have a wealth of resources that is invaluable to adults. They can show grown-ups how to live in the moment, how to have a sense of wonder, how to be more creative, enthusiastic, spontaneous, and playful. <u>Growing Down</u>, in the tradition of <u>All I Really Need to Know I Learned in Kindergarten</u>, is for the increasing discontented population who have more but are enjoying it less.

<u>How Do You Spell Relief?: Five Keys to Increase Your Laugh Life</u>

In my seminars nationwide, I present the five key letters (L-A-U-G-H) to help audiences get more laughter and less stress in their life and their work. With lively stories and fun-filled exercises, this book presents that system.

<u>The Red Nose Book: How a Little Clown Nose Can Make a Big Difference</u>
Every audience member in my presentation gets to take home a red sponge-rubber clown nose. Over the years these audience members have shared how this small prop has made a big difference in their life. <u>The Red Nose Book</u> will contain some of their fascinating/funny stories along with other red clown nose facts and anecdotes.

•••

Chapter-by-Chapter Outline

PROLOGUE
HUMOR: POWER IN A POWERLESS SITUATION

*"You cannot prevent the birds of sorrow from flying over head,
but you can prevent them from making nests in your hair."*
Chinese Proverb

<u>The Courage to Laugh</u> begins by reminding the reader that, like the proverb above, they don't have to give a home to their "birds of sorrow." They can look for the lighter side of their life-threatening situations and not allow their suffering to make nests in their hair.

The prologue asks: "Are life-threatening situations too serious for humor?" It answers this question by discussing the benefits of humor during these times. It shows how humor can ease death-related fears, help people cope, give them hope, and aid in communicating at a time when coping is often difficult, hope nonexistent, and communication at a standstill.

PART I
LEARNING TO LAUGH FROM THOSE WHO KNOW

Chapter 1- Ha-Ha Hospital Humor
Question: Who was the guy who invented hospital gowns?
Answer: Seymour Butts.

The first chapter provides examples of how patients have made their hospital stay more palatable by poking fun at it.

A classical example comes from Norman Cousins, author of <u>Anatomy of An Illness</u>, who believed that it is the responsibility of the patient to not only cheer himself up but the hospital staff as well. When a nurse asked for a urine sample, Cousins filled the jar with apple juice. Upon her return, Cousins held the jar up to the light and said, "This looks a bit cloudy." Then just before he gulped it down, he declared, "I think we need to recycle it."

Chapter 2- Hospice Humor: Serious, Yes... Solemn, No!
"If I ever needed humor it is now." - Hospice patient

One hospice patient told me that she didn't want to eat anymore. Several days later she came down to the breakfast table and was eating up a storm. When questioned about the sudden turn of events, she replied smugly, "Well after all, nobody wants to die on an empty stomach."

At times, I have felt like dying while in the midst of a horrible flu. I have also had several operations, including a serious mastoid in the pre-penicillin days of my childhood. But as an adult I have never been in a situation where my life-span was seriously threatened because of illness. So I don't know if I would be able to laugh, like the hospice patient above, under such circumstances. I have, however, worked with and read about how those facing imminent death and loss have done so. Their stories are contained in this chapter.

Chapter 3-- The C Words-- Cancer & Comedy
"Cancer Schmancer, as long as your healthy!" - Jewish saying

Mirthful and motivational stories, cartoons and poems from those who have lived or are living and laughing with cancer including such celebrities as Linda Ellerbee and Gilda Radner. (This was one of Allen's sample chapters.)

Chapter 4- AIDS Ain't Funny... or Is It?
"You think you have to hold back your craziness, but when you're sick you can let it out in all its garish colors." - Anatole Broyard

In a wonderful book about the final days of his life after he was diagnosed with prostate cancer, Anatole Broyard writes in Intoxicated by My Illness, that "a critical illness is like a great permission, an authorization or absolving. It's all right for a threatened man to be romantic, even crazy, if he feels like it. All your life," Broyard continues, "you think you have to hold back your craziness, but when you're sick you can let it out in all its garish colors."

Broyard did not have AIDS nor was he writing about the gay and lesbian community, but he could have very well been doing so. This group of people has been letting out all their garish and glorious colors for years by using humor as a weapon against oppressors. They courageously continue to do so against their most recent and devastating enemy, AIDS. This chapter contains their inspiring stories.

Chapter 5- Kids-- Great Wisdom from Small Fry
"You can learn to control your mind and decide to be happy 'inside' with a smiling heart, in spite of what happens to you on the 'outside'."
- Written by a child with cancer

When Erma Bombeck was doing research for her book about children surviving cancer, she said "I felt like I was the innocent child and they were the adults, dispensing wisdom." Kids have a way of dealing with illness in a much lighter way than adults. Because of this, they can be an encouraging resource for terminally ill adults who are looking for ways to lighten up their own predicament.

The stories in this chapter come from many sources including kids with cancer, Bernie Siegel, Erma Bombeck and Wavy Gravy.

Chapter 6- Lingering Death- Alzheimer's, Disability, Incarceration

"Nothing, no experience good or bad, no belief, no cause, is in itself momentous enough to monopolize the whole of life to the exclusion of laughter."
-   Alfred North Whitehead

This chapter focuses on examples of humor from those confronting the death-related issue of a curtailed life. It contains stories about such things as Alzheimer's disease, disabilities, and imprisonment.

One woman, for example, saw a bit of the bright side to her husband forgetting things because of his Alzheimer's disease. She said, "He forgets he's married. Every morning he proposes to me."

Chapter 7- Sudden Death- Disasters, Suicide, War

Razors pain you/Rivers are damp/Acids stain you/And drugs cause cramp/Guns aren't lawful/Nooses give/Gas smells awful/You might as well live.
-   Dorothy Parker

Minutes after the disasters of Chernobyl and the Challenger space shuttle there were jokes crossing the county. Dark, black, macabre jokes, but jokes nonetheless.

This chapter explains why we kid around about such atrocities. It also provides examples of humor in such unlikely places as disasters, suicide and war.

One man in my workshop provided me with some disaster humor after the major earthquake in San Francisco several years ago. The man came home from work just as the earth started to shake and a portion of his porch roof collapsed. His seven-year-old son came running out of the house yelling, "I didn't do it. I didn't do it. I didn't do it."

PART II
SEEING DEMISE THRU HUMOROUS EYES

Part II contains lessons in learning to laugh about life/death situations from those who lives may not be threatened but who have significant insights nonetheless.

Chapter 8- Lessons from Caregivers

"Somberness won't make you or your loved one feel any better."

— Rabbi Earl Grollman

Hospice volunteers, families/friends taking care of a dying loved one, and professional caregivers frequently encounter situational humor. Their amusing and amazing anecdotes are shared in this chapter.

One oncology nurse, for example, uses playful bantering to ease a patient's nervousness. When one of them asks her how many times has she done a certain procedure before, she replies, "Oh, I actually work in housekeeping but they were a little short staffed up here today, so...."

Chapter 9- Lessons from Other Cultures /Religions

"Does your heart ache? Laugh it off." - Jewish Folk-saying

This chapter begins by exploring the less-serious view that several cultures take toward death and dying. It touches on the boisterous Irish wake, Mexico's joyous Day of the Dead, and a raucous Balinese cremation ceremony. The main focus of the chapter, however, is on how the Jewish and Zen religions use their wit and wisdom to teach death-related subjects.

Chapter 10- Lessons from Popular Culture

"Death is always with us; creative art helps us know it, live with it and even laugh at it." - Dr. Robert Litman

This chapter discusses how cartoonists, comedians, movies and TV shows poke fun at death and as a result help relieve our death-related fears.

It first provides examples from some well-known comedians and cartoonists. The illustrations come from such talents as cartoonists S. Gross and S. Harris, and, comedians George Carlin and Woody Allen ("I don't believe in an afterlife, but I'm bringing a change of underwear just in case.")

It next looks at how some television shows and movies explore the lighter side of life-threatening situations. Examples come from such movies as "Steel Magnolias", "The Wedding", and TV's "Northern Exposure".

Finally, the chapter ends by taking a brief look at the close, but not so obvious, connection between the clown, that frequent source of delight, and the grim reaper, that frequent source of dread. (This was one of Allen's sample chapters.)

PART III
TO DIE LAUGHING

"To weep too much for the dead is to affront the living." - Old Proverb

The last section of <u>The Courage to Laugh</u> focuses on how survivors use humor to ease their loss. And, finally, to end the book, there is a collection of funny quips and quotes about death and dying.

Chapter 11- Mirth & Mourning
"They say such nice things about people at their funerals. It is a shame that I am going to miss mine by only a few days." - Garrison Keillor

This chapter provides examples of how survivors focus on the joyous memories of loved ones and on the celebrations of life they created in memory of the deceased.

The scattering of the ashes for the slain gay San Francisco supervisor Harvey Milk is one example. His ashes were wrapped in Doonesbury comics and R.I.P. was spelled out in rhinestones across the box. When friends scattered the ashes into the ocean, they also tossed in some purple Kool-aid and bubble bath. Milk left, in an appropriately fitting finale for a gay man, in a bubbly bath of lavender.

The chapter ends with examples of humorous last words and comic tombstone epitaphs. An example of the former is what Oscar Wilde was reported to have uttered on his deathbed: "This wallpaper is terrible. One of us has to go." An example of the latter, tombstone humor, is "See I told you I was very sick!".

Chapter 12-- Wise & Witty Words
"For three days after death, hair and finger nails continue to grow but phone calls taper off." - Johnny Carson

The final chapter proves that death and dying <u>can</u> be a laughing matter. It provides an assortment of quips, quotes and anecdotes ranging from the sick bed to the grave... and beyond. Example:

A comic named "Professor Backwards" specialty was pronouncing words and sentences in reverse. He was mugged one day and died as a result of the injuries sustained in the attack. Comedian Chevy Chase reported the incident by noting: "Passersby ignored Professor Backwards' cries of 'Pleh! Pleh!'"

Epilogue
THE LAST LAUGH

"In the end, everything is a gag."   -   Charlie Chaplin

The Courage to Laugh leaves the reader with an powerful tale from the Talmud. It reminds them that "when a child is born, all rejoice; when someone dies, all weep. But it makes just as much sense, if not more, to rejoice at the end of a life as at the beginning. For no one can tell what events await a newborn child, but when a mortal dies he has successfully completed a journey."

•••

*If the doctor told me I only had six
minutes to live, I'd type a little faster.*

- Isaac Asimov

APPENDIX

Here is a simple script you can follow when you call magazine editors:

RING, RING!!!

Editor: Fred Prinstone.
You: Hi Fred, Charlotte Arthur here. You don't know me, but I am looking to hire a collaborator on a project about _____. Is this an okay time for a two minute conversation?
If Fred says no, then ask when a good time to speak would be.
Editor: I've got two minutes now. But that's all I have.
You: No problem, I promise not to take longer than that. At any rate, I have _____ years experience as a _____ and I am looking to hire an experienced writer or editor to write a book with me.
Is that a task you would consider taking on?
At this point, the editor will usually ask you more about the book and whether you have a publisher. Explain the concept of your book, and if you are going the traditional publisher route, the process of writing a book proposal. Eventually, you will need to ask if this is a project he would be interested in. If he says yes, make an appointment to have further phone conversations or to meet in person. If he says no, say the following:
You: That's okay. I knew you might be too busy. Say, you deal with a lot of writers. Do you know someone who might be a good person to call for this project?
At this point, if you're lucky, the editor will give you a name. If it's just one name say, "Why'd you pick her?" After he explains, say "Who else?"
Repeat these questions with each name he gives until he runs out of names.
If he gives you a list of names all at once, ask him who he would call first, and why. Then ask who he would call next, etc.

WHEN THE EDITOR ASKS HOW YOU GOT HIS NAME:

- If you already have a sample of the magazine and his work, mention that. (And say how much you like it)
- If your search is for a local editor of a small circulation magazine, tell him that.
- If you have chosen to look for Canadian writers, say "because of the exchange rate, I thought I would start my search with editors of Canadian magazines."

- If you are looking for someone in the United States but outside the region you live in, say ."I'm calling editors of small magazines that I found in Writer's Market."

IF THE EDITOR ASKS ABOUT YOUR BUDGET:

Don't answer this question directly. You want the editor to become enthusiastic about the project before you negotiate. You also may need to educate him on the publishing business (royalties, book advances, credits, etc.) and the doors that a published book will open for him.

> "There are an awful lot of variables involved in discussing that. Why don't we talk further, and see if there's a match between us. If there is, I am sure we can come to some kind of agreement that works reasonably well for both of us."

You might want to add, "What kind of fee do you have in mind?" to make sure he's a reasonable match

CALLING A FREELANCE WRITER:

The only difference between calling a magazine editor and a freelance writer is how you start the call. With the freelance writer, you get to mention how you were referred to her. The call starts like this:

You: Hi, is Frieda there?
Freelancer: This is Frieda.
You: Hi Frieda, this is Charlotte Arthur. You don't know me, but _____ gave me your name. I am looking for a collaborator for a writing project about _____. Is this a good time for a two-minute conversation?

Then continue the conversation as described above.

CALLING FUTURE EXPERTS:

If you are asking a Future Expert to work on spec, explain how that works early in the phone call. It's not fair to let him think he will definitely be paid if that's not true. But do a good job selling him the value ghostwriting a published book can bring to his career as a writer. See the section on Quid Pro Quo, p. 25, for details you can mention.

BIBLIOGRAPHY

Bain, Donald. *Every Midget Has an Uncle Sam Costume: Writing For a Living*. Fort Lee: Barricade Books, 2002.

Bennett, Hal Zina with Michael Larsen. *How to Write With a Collaborator*. Cincinnati: Writer's Digest Books, 1988.

Bly, Robert W. *How to Get Your Book Published: The Inside Secrets of a Successful Author*. White Plains: Roblin Press, 1997.

Caples, John. *Tested Advertising Methods*. New York: Harper & Brothers, 1932.

Herman, Deborah Levine with Cynthia Black. *Spiritual Writing: From Inspiration to Publication*. Hillsboro: Beyond Words Publishing, Inc., 2002.

Herman, Jeff. *You Can Make it Big Writing Books: A Top Agent Shows You How to Develop a Million-Dollar Bestseller*. Roseville: Prima Publishing, 1999.

Herman Jeff and Deborah M. Adams. *Write the Perfect Book Proposals: 10 Proposals That Sold and Why*. New York: John Wiley & Sons, Inc., 1993.

Howry, Michelle. *Agents, Editors, and You: The Insider's Guide to Getting Your Book Published*. Cincinnati: Writer's Digest Books, 2002.

Jenkins, Jerrold R. with Mardi Link. *Inside the Best Sellers*. Traverse City: Rhodes and Easton, 1997.

Jenkins, Jerrold R. and Anne M. Stanton. *Publish to Win: Smart Strategies to Sell More Books*. Traverse City: Rhodes and Easton, 1997.

Levinson, Jay Conrad, Rick Frishman and Michael Larsen. *Guerrilla Marketing for Writers: 100 Weapons for Selling Your Work*. Cincinnati: Writer's Digest Books, 2001.

Lyon, Elizabeth. *Nonfiction Book Proposals Anybody Can Write*. New York: The Berkley Publishing Group, 1995.

Mandell, Judy. *Book Editors Talk to Writers*. New York: John Wiley & Sons, Inc., 1995.

Page, Susan. *The Shortest Distance Between You and a Published Book: Everything You Need to Know in the Order You Need to Know It*. New York: Broadway Books, 1997.

Poynter, Dan. *The Self-Publishing Manual: How to Write, Print and Sell Your Own Book.* Santa Barbara: Para Publishing, 1979.

Poynter, Dan and Mindy Bingham. *Is There a Book Inside You? Writing Alone or With a Collaborator.* Santa Barbara: Para Publishing, 1985.

Ross, Tom and Marilyn. *The Complete Guide to Self-Publishing: Everything You Need to Know to Write, Publish, Promote and Sell Your Own Book.* Cincinnati: Writer's Digest Books, 2002.

Rubie, Peter. *Writer's Market FAQs: Fast Answers About Getting Published and the Business of Writing.* Cincinnati: Writer's Digest Books, 2002.

Rubie, Peter. *The Everything Get Published Book.* New York: Adams Business Media, 2000.

Stine, Jean Marie. *Writing Successful Self-Help & How-To Books: An Insider's Guide to Everything You Need to Know.* New York: John Wiley & Sons, Inc., 1997.

INDEX

Mahesh Grossman

ABOUT THE AUTHOR

Mahesh Grossman has been called a "ghostwriting guru" by the Salt Lake Tribune and "America's leading expert on ghostwriting" by Jim Christoferson of KWKC-AM.

Grossman was the ghostwriter on books published by Putnam and Crown and has been involved in the development of six others as ghostwriter or editor. He has appeared on over 100 radio and television stations: Audiences enjoy his tales of ghostwriting as it relates to American history as well as sordid tidbits about greedy authors and vengeful ghostwriters. Best of all, they come away with knowledge of how to hire a ghostwriter to write their tales, no matter what their budget.

Grossman, a graduate of Columbia University, is also nationally known for his teleseminars on "How to Get a Six-Figure Book Advance".

He is president of The Authors Team (http://www.AuthorsTeam.com), a firm that turns "credible experts into Incredible Authors" through ghostwriting, editing, and coaching. The Authors Team also offers publishing and distribution to bookstores nationwide.

Grossman resides in Santa Cruz with his wife and daughter.

My free e-zine, Author Secrets, includes tips on finding an agent, getting published, self-publishing, and publicizing and marketing your book. To sign up for a free subscription, send an e-mail to <u>GetPublished@AuthorsTeam.com</u> with the word "list" on the subject line.

Quick Order Form

Fax orders: 831-458-1501. Send this form

Telephone orders: Call 1-866-7-AUTHOR toll free. Have your credit card ready.

email orders: GetPublished@AuthorsTeam.com

Please send me additional copies of *Write a Book Without Lifting a Finger*. I understand that I may return any of them for a full refund-for any reason, no questions asked.

Number of Copies_____@ $19.95 each

Please send more FREE information on:

☐ Other Books   ☐ Speaking/Seminars
☐ Mailing Lists   ☐ Consulting

Name:_____

Address:_____

City:_____State:_____ Zip:_____

Telephone:_____

email address:_____

Sales tax: Please add 8% for products shipped to California addresses.

Shipping by air: U.S.: $4.00 for first book and $2.00 for each additional.
International: $9.00 for first book; $5.00 for each additional.

Payment: ☐ Check ☐ Credit card:
☐ Visa   ☐ MasterCard   ☐ Optima   ☐ AMEX   ☐ Discover

Card number:_____

Name on card:_____Exp. date:_____

We give discounts for orders of 10 or more books. Call 866-7-AUTHOR for details.